Invisible Abuse

Instantly spot the covert deception and manipulation tactics of narcissists

Kara Lawrence

© Copyright 2019 - All rights reserved.

It is not legal to reproduce, duplicate, or transmit any part of this document in either electronic means or in printed format. Recording of this publication is strictly prohibited and any storage of this document is not allowed unless with written permission from the publisher except for the use of brief quotations in a book review.

While every precaution has been taken in the preparation of this book, the publisher assumes no responsibility for errors or omissions, or for damages resulting from the use of the information contained herein.

INVISIBLE ABUSE

First edition. November 9, 2019.

Copyright © 2019 Kara Lawrence.

Written by Kara Lawrence.

Table of Contents

Invisible Abuse
    Table of Contents
    Introduction
    Chapter One: Who is the Narcissist?
    Chapter Two: Are You Suffering from Narcissistic Abuse Syndrome?
    Chapter Three: How to Spot a Narcissist
    Chapter Four: Disarming the Narcissist
    Chapter Five: Empaths and Narcissists
    Chapter Six: Is My Mother a Narcissist?
    Chapter Seven: No Contact
    Chapter Eight: Beginning Recovery
    Chapter Nine: Alternative Therapies
    Chapter Ten: Learning to Change Patterns and Protect Yourself
    Final Words
    References

Introduction

Do you feel alone or abandoned even when you are in a relationship? Are you worried that your partner is only putting up with you? Do you ever feel like you are not good enough?

Do you ever feel that the person you fell in love with is not the same person you are with today? Where did the charm and charisma go? Are you in a relationship where you are being controlled even down to what you wear or eat? In fact, you feel that the relationship has gotten abusive, but you are too afraid to say anything because you might be punished or ignored.

If you feel this way, you might be dealing with a narcissist.

What is a narcissist?

A narcissist, or person with Narcissistic Personality Disorder, is a person who falls on the spectrum of being narcissistic. People with this mental illness have an inflated sense of superiority. They believe they are the most important person in the room; require a lot of attention; lack empathy for other people; and demand that people treat them as being superior to others. Moreover, people with Narcissistic Personality Disorder often become abusive towards others and try to control people that they feel are below them.

If you feel like you are always walking on eggshells around your partner, or your partner constantly belittles you and makes you feel undeserving, you may be suffering from Narcissistic Abuse Syndrome.

However, you have taken the first step towards recovery: seeking the truth. Narcissists will assert their reality onto you, clouding your judgment of what is normal and healthy behavior. The purpose of this book is to unravel the web that their influence has spun, give you clear insight into the condition, and offer recommendations on how to heal from the trauma and prevent it from happening again.

There was a time in my life where I was always trying to prove myself to my narcissistic mother and later, a partner who had the same narcissistic characteristics as my mother. I suffered needlessly for years, constantly doubting myself and exhausting myself by putting my efforts towards achieving an unattainable goal that the narcissist in my life was constantly rewriting (though I didn't know this at the time).

Eventually, the abuse became more serious. I began to believe that I was inferior to other people, my narcissistic partner in particular. This plunged me into a deep depression where I lost all my will to live. I was totally isolated from my friends and family because that was how my narcissistic partner controlled me. Everything I did was wrong and made my partner unhappy. When I was at my lowest point, I called a helpline, and this started my journey of recovery. Once I knew what I was dealing with, I was able to get the help that I needed.

With knowledge of Narcissistic Personality Disorder and a few simple tools under my belt, I was able to identify four steps in order to heal from narcissistic abuse:

1. Identify the problem - hint: it is NOT your fault!

2. Separate from the abusive individual - this can be difficult, but this book offers tips to help.

3. Heal from trauma - we will go over several popular techniques and some unorthodox ones.

4. Avoid repeating the cycle! Defend yourself in the future from the same type of abuse over and over again.

Through the implementation of this process, I was able to recover fully from the trauma of abuse and seek out healthy and supportive relationships. Ultimately, I found my current partner, someone I can be around without judging or questioning myself.

After my recovery, I began to study this mental illness so that I could help others who were similarly abused. This book is the culmination of my research and personal experiences with people suffering from Narcissistic Personality Disorder.

Every day that you remain in a relationship with someone who has Narcissistic Personality Disorder is a day that you are in danger of losing yourself. The abusive individual, whether he or she knows it, is covertly selling you the idea that you are not good enough; that you are the problem in the relationship; and that things would be better if you would only change.

But by starting your journey of recovery, you have put yourself on the road to freedom from the shackles of narcissistic emotional abuse. Be confident that with the right knowledge at your fingertips, followed by the appropriate actions, you, too, can make a full recovery and escape abusive relationships.

No longer will the person with Narcissistic Personality Disorder be able to abuse you emotionally or psychologically; you will recognize the signs of manipulation and know how to take that power away from them. By understanding what Narcissistic Personality Disorder is, you will be able to step up and control your own life.

The first step to a newer, healthier, more confident you involves arming yourself with the knowledge compiled for you in the following pages. But equally important are the actions you must follow, which are also outlined ahead.

The more you know about Narcissistic Personality Disorder, the sooner you will be able to start your recovery. In this book, you will find the knowledge that will set you free. Don't be afraid to change your life for the better. Take a deep breath and dive right in!

Chapter One: Who is the Narcissist?

After years of searching for The One, you finally found someone who connects with you. He's handsome, intelligent, and seems to be really into you. You have a whirlwind courtship; you've never been treated this well before. Before you know it, you're a couple, and all of your dreams have come true: You've found your perfect love.

This sounds like the beginning of a fairy tale - lonely woman finds a perfect man. But while it might have started out like a fairy tale, it doesn't end like one. Out of nowhere, the person you fell in love with begins demeaning you. He makes you feel guilty about things you didn't do. He flaunts his intelligence and makes you feel foolish. Stop acting so ignorant, he says. You stop going to Mensa meetings in fear of being humiliated.

Last night, he said some things that made you question his intelligence. Quietly, you start to suspect that he isn't very clever, though he seems to think he is. He tells you every day that you aren't worthy of someone as important as he is. You should feel lucky he's still willing to be with you. Saturday evening, at the party, he pulls you aside while you were talking to Jimmy. Get with the program, he quietly seethes.

Jimmy is witty, and you miss that in a partner. On the way home, you make the mistake of saying you enjoyed the party. You mention that Jimmy was really witty and smart, and he falls into a rage, screaming at you. You should worship *him* and no one else! He slaps you when you open your mouth to say something. Your cheek stings. You've bitten your tongue, and it's bleeding.

He doesn't care.

He drives on like nothing happened. He says that everyone is jealous of him. People wish they were him. Watch your behavior, he warns you, because there are dozens of women dying to be with him.

This scenario has happened to many women. They fall in love with a narcissist, and their life is turned upside down. Their confidence is blown, and they lose the ability to walk away. Being in a relationship with a narcissist is worse than an addiction. It's like being in a funhouse with blurry mirrors - you lose your unique sense of reality and fall into that of the narcissist.

Are you in a relationship like this? Are you in love with a narcissist?

Let's examine the definition of a narcissist.

The Narcissist

A true narcissist is a person who thinks that he is better than everyone else on the planet. This person needs to be told frequently that he is unique and just about perfect. He needs to be admired for all his qualities, whether real or imagined. When something happens to you, he does not connect with your situation and cannot empathize with you. He will hurt your feelings a million times over and never care. If your dog dies, it will not affect him at all. You never see an ounce of feeling. If this sounds like your partner, I'm sorry to say that you are involved with a narcissist.

The person you are with is a textbook case of narcissism. He has a "pervasive pattern of grandiosity" (American Psychiatric Association, 2013); needs to be admired in everything that he does; and has a total lack of empathy.

You might be in denial about the narcissist in your life, so I want to help you understand this illness and think about breaking away. Leaving will be hard, but it can be done, and the more you know, the better equipped you will be when that time comes. Hence, we'll start from the beginning and learn exactly what a narcissistic personality is.

What Is an Overt Narcissist?

The overt narcissist is a person who is open about narcissistic. There is nothing ambiguous about this type of person; he stands out in a crowd. The overt narcissist is a person whose life revolves around grandiosity. While he may appear humble at first, his humility is an act that hides intense ambitions, extravagant behaviors, and an unwavering belief in his own infallibility.

If you have a relationship with the overt narcissist, it will be a shallow one. An overt narcissist seeks your total attention but is dissatisfied when he receives it. He is charming but secretly insecure, and hence always preoccupied with appearances. While he may make a big show about having no respect for money, deep inside, he longs for wealth and superiority. He has questionable morals, and he exaggerates modesty. You cannot criticize an overt narcissist without him lashing out in response.

You might be impressed with an overt narcissist's arrogance, but he doesn't come by his knowledge the usual way. Overt narcissists take shortcuts in learning about things. They are very opinionated, decisive, and expect others to believe as they do. Most importantly, an overt narcissist cannot empathize with others. In short, overt narcissists have an egocentric perception of reality (Phatack, 2018).

What Is a Covert Narcissist?

A covert narcissist is a person who conceals his narcissism. You cannot see him coming like you can an overt narcissist. The covert narcissist is aimless; his interest in things superficial and amateurish. He seems knowledgeable, but when it comes to the finer points of a subject, he doesn't have a clue.

When you first meet the covert narcissist, he appears shy, lacking in self-confidence, and full of self-doubt. You might even find him sweet. But as your relationship with him develops, you realize that he lives in a world of his own, one you cannot access. The covert narcissist is selfish, and although the two of you are partners, he cares too much about himself to ever pay any attention to your needs.

You see, the covert narcissist craves power and glory. He envies others for their possessions, relationships, and talents and masks his insecurity and jealousy with an overzealous self-defense. Don't you dare apply any criticism because even a long sigh will provoke the covert narcissist. The covert narcissist trusts only himself. Any question, no matter the intent, is an attack on his self-esteem, and the covert narcissist will change his reality as a response to your imaginary attack (Phatak, 2018).

There is no way you can ever understand a person like the narcissist, who is governed by his own issues of wanting to possess power, prestige, and personal adequacy (Kartha, 2018). This book will discuss the covert narcissist.

What is NPD?

People throw around the label narcissistic indiscriminately in today's society. If someone takes too many selfies, we think to ourselves, *What a narcissist*. If someone admires themselves in excess, we label them as narcissistic. However, a true narcissist has a mental illness and fulfills distinct criteria.

Narcissistic personality disorder (NPD) is a mental condition in which a person has an inflated sense of self; a deep need for attention and admiration; no empathy for anyone else; and troubled relationships (Kassel, 2019).

There is no black and white test for determining if someone has NPD. In fact, when describing the disorder, psychologists use the term *spectrum*, indicating that the disorder consists of a range of linked conditions. Someone on the lower end of the spectrum may not seem a narcissist, while someone on the higher end will show most, if not all, the characteristics of a narcissist. The spectrum will also indicate the intensity of the characteristics shown. If a narcissist is on the low range of the spectrum, it might be hard for you to recognize that he is a narcissist. He might, for example, seem entitled, but only occasionally so. Yet if the narcissist is on the higher range of the spectrum, he will be very intense - you will easily spot his sense of privilege.

According to the Diagnostic and Statistical Manual of Mental Disorders (DSM-5), there are currently five characteristics of NPD persons. Most important are criteria regarding personality functioning and any pathological traits as stated below. A person with NPD will have:

A. Significant impairments in personality functioning manifest by both:

1. Impairments in self functioning (a or b):

a. *Identity*: Excessive reference to others for self-definition and self-esteem regulation; exaggerated self-appraisal may be inflated or deflated, or vacillate between extremes; emotional regulation mirrors fluctuations in self-esteem.

b. *Self-direction*: Goal-setting is based on gaining approval from others; personal standards are unreasonably high in order to see oneself as exceptional, or too low based on a sense of entitlement; often unaware of own motivations.

2. Impairments in interpersonal functioning (a or b):

a. *Empathy*: Impaired ability to recognize or identify with the feelings and needs of others; excessively attuned to reactions of others, but only if perceived as relevant to self; over- or underestimate of own effect on others.

b. *Intimacy:* Relationships largely superficial and exist to serve self-esteem regulation; mutuality constrained by little genuine interest in others' experiences and predominance of a need for personal gain

B. Pathological personality traits in the following domain:

1. Antagonism, characterized by:

a. *Grandiosity*: Feelings of entitlement, either overt or covert; self-centeredness; firmly holding to the belief that one is better than others; condescending toward others

b. *Attention seeking*: Excessive attempts to attract and be the focus of the attention of others; admiration seeking (American Psychiatric Association, 2013)

In addition, "the impairments in personality functioning and the individual's personality trait expression are relatively stable across time and consistent across situations; the impairments in personality functioning and the individual's personality trait expression are not better understood as normative for the individual's developmental stage or socio-cultural environment; the impairments in personality functioning and the individual's personality trait expression are not solely due to the direct physiological effects of a substance (e.g., a drug of abuse, medication) or a general medical condition (e.g., severe head trauma)" (American Psychiatric Association, 2013).

Persons with NPD may also have tendencies towards the following, though these are no longer recognized by the American Psychiatric Association (APA) as official criteria for diagnosis:

1. a grandiose sense of self-importance excessive reference to others for self-definition and self-esteem regulation
2. preoccupation with fantasies of unlimited success, power, brilliance, beauty, or ideal love

3. belief that they are special and unique and can only be understood by, or should associate with, other special or high-status people or institutions
4. a need for excessive admiration
5. a sense of entitlement
6. interpersonally exploitative behavior
7. lack of empathy
8. envy of others or a belief that others are envious of them
9. a demonstration of arrogant and haughty behaviors or attitudes (APA, 2000)

It is hard for an untrained individual to diagnosis a person with NPD, especially if you are in a romantic relationship with him or her. It is more effective to analyze your relationship to see if it is a healthy one. Over time, you might begin to see behavior that sends up a red flag.

What Is a Sociopath?

In an effort to understand NPD, let's look at what NPD isn't and examine sociopathic and psychotic behaviors. A sociopath is a person diagnosed with antisocial personality disorder (ASPD). People with ASPD do not understand the feelings of others, and they tend to break rules or make impulsive decisions without feeling consequential guilt. More often than not, a sociopath will be charismatic and charming (Jewell, 2018).

The DSM-5 lists traits that a person with ASPD may display. To be diagnosed with ASPD, a person over the age of 18 must show:

A. Significant impairments in personality functioning manifest by:

1. Impairments in self functioning (a or b):

a. *Identity*: Ego-centrism; self-esteem derived from personal gain, power, or pleasure.

b. *Self-direction*: Goal-setting based on personal gratification; absence of prosocial internal standards associated with failure to conform to lawful or culturally normative ethical behavior.

2. Impairments in interpersonal functioning (a or b):

a. *Empathy*: Lack of concern for feelings, needs, or suffering of others; lack of remorse after hurting or mistreating another.

b. *Intimacy*: Incapacity for mutually intimate relationships, as exploitation is a primary means of relating to others, including by deceit and coercion; use of dominance or intimidation to control others.

B. Pathological personality traits in the following domains:

1. Antagonism, characterized by:

a. *Manipulativeness*: Frequent use of subterfuge to influence or control others; use of seduction, charm, glibness, or ingratiation to achieve one's ends.

b. *Deceitfulness*: Dishonesty and fraudulence; misrepresentation of self; embellishment or fabrication when relating events.

c. *Callousness*: Lack of concern for feelings or problems of others; lack of guilt or remorse about the negative or harmful effects of one's actions on others; aggression; sadism.

d. *Hostility*: Persistent or frequent angry feelings; anger or irritability in response to minor slights and insults; mean, nasty, or vengeful behavior.

2. Disinhibition, characterized by:

a. *Irresponsibility*: Disregard for – and failure to honor – financial and other obligations or commitments; lack of respect for – and lack of follow through on – agreements and promises.

b. *Impulsivity*: Acting on the spur of the moment in response to immediate stimuli; acting on a momentary basis without a plan or consideration of outcomes; difficulty establishing and following plans.

c. *Risk taking*: Engagement in dangerous, risky, and potentially self-damaging activities, unnecessarily and without regard for consequences; boredom proneness and thoughtless initiation of activities to counter boredom; lack of concern for one's limitations and denial of the reality of personal danger (APA, 2013)

As with other personality disorders, any impairments must be consistent, un-normative for the individual's life stage and environment, and not the sole result of any substance abuse or medical conditions (APA, 2013).

There are other traits of ADSP: not showing emotions, being manipulative, and having a sense of superiority and strong, unwavering opinions. People with ADSP do not learn from their mistakes, and they do not develop positive friendships or relationships. They like to take control by intimidating and threatening people, and they are apt to using mind games to obtain this control. Further, those with ADSP have a likelihood of performing frequent criminal acts, taking risks, threatening suicide, and developing an addiction to drugs or other prohibited substances.

A person with ADPD can be diagnosed as early as 15 years old if they show the following symptoms:

- breaking rules without regard for the consequences
- needlessly destroying things that belong to themselves or others
- stealing
- lying or constantly deceiving others
- being aggressive towards others or animals (Jewell, 2018)

When determining if you are involved with a narcissist, it is important to understand what a sociopath is as the two conditions are often confused.

What Is the Difference between a Sociopath and a Psychopath?

Is there a difference between a sociopath and a psychopath? The truth is that both of these disorders refer to people with ASPD, and both disorders can be genetic or learned. Instead of finding clinical differences between the two conditions, people distinguish them by the severity of the symptoms.

A sociopath is believed to be less dangerous than a psychopath. The sociopath does not significantly disrupt the lives of other people. A psychopath, on the other hand, is considered very dangerous. As stated above, however, both sociopaths and psychopaths show symptomatic behavior that fits the ASPD profile.

The Difference between ASPD and NPD

The distinguishing quality between a person with ASPD and one with NPD is that a person with NPD bases his life on the imagined judgment of others. He may not have any empathy, similar to a psychopath or sociopath, but he reacts to the way people feel about him. A person with NPD fits into society, whereas a psychopath or sociopath does not fit in and likely does not even care to do so.

A person with NPD rarely, if ever, shows aggressive or aggravated behavior. He is not known for getting into fights or having a powerful desire to hurt people. The narcissist has an intense need for attention and admiration. He may be controlling, but only in private - he is socially mindful. The person with NPD feels special to society and looks for other superior individuals. He may never find that person as his sense of self is exaggerated, but regardless, he will make known that he belongs to a special category of superior people.

A person with ASPD, on the other hand, will act out and do what he pleases no matter how damaging his behavior is to others. If he is controlling in private, he will also be controlling in public. The person with ASPD does not care about social norms or boundaries.

While ASPD and NPD are both characterized by a lack of empathy towards others, they are two separate mental disorders.

Chapter Summary

- There are two types of narcissists: overt and covert
- A covert narcissist hides his narcissism when entering relationships
- People with ASPD are different than people with NPD

In the next chapter, you will learn about the signs of being in a relationship with a covert narcissist.

Chapter Two: Are You Suffering from Narcissistic Abuse Syndrome?

It's a tough world out there if you're looking for a relationship. Social media and dating apps are front and center in our lives, but it's still hard to meet strangers and let your guard down. How do you know she's reliable? Her neighbors swear she's a good person, but can you trust them?

Ideally, you'd meet someone through your family or friend network who has been vouched for. He's friends with your cousin, so he has to be a good person, right? Yet being vouched for isn't always a guarantee that the person will be good to you. In fact, you might find yourself with a person whose sense of reality is warped and distorted while outwardly seeming affable and generous. You might find a covert narcissist.

In the beginning of a relationship with a covert narcissist, things may seem like a dream. You are treated like a princess. But eventually, the midnight clock tolls; your carriage turns back into a pumpkin, and your glass slipper shatters. The person you've fallen in love with has become your abuser instead of your lover.

You find that you no longer have a keen sense of self. Your self-confidence has diminished to the point that you do not recognize yourself. You strive to break up before things get worse, but you are "hoovered" - lured back into the relationship by a lover with crocodile tears that pierce your heart. Yet after a few days, your lover is back to his old tricks.

Narcissistic Abuse

Narcissistic Abuse Syndrome is a serious form of abuse that can occur when you are in a relationship with a person who has narcissistic personality disorder (NPD) - a relationship that goes from bliss to psychological violence in an instant.

A person who has covert NPD moves into your life in such a stealthy manner that you have no warning before finding yourself on the receiving end of verbal and emotional abuse. Your partner projects himself and his toxic weaknesses onto you. He stonewalls and sabotages you, and he devises smear campaigns that wipe out your dignity.

While your partner undermines you, all you see on your end is a cold and entitled person who lacks empathy and awareness of how he hurt you. The person with covert NPD can only think about himself. He never considers the possibility that he is the cause of your overwhelming unhappiness. This is what Narcissistic Abuse looks like.

The Many Facets of Abuse

The most striking trait of Narcissistic Abuse Syndrome is that while it is happening, you do not recognize it as abuse. The person with NPD is so skilled at twisting reality for her own means: After a terrible fight, your NPD partner love bombs you, and you forgive her and think that maybe you are acting foolish. You feel guilty because the NPD person makes you believe everything was your fault. She portrays herself as perfect and incapable of doing something as low as abuse. You're the one who overreacted and started the fight.

Yet after months of fights and situations like the one above, you find that you are suffering from symptoms of PTSD. You find that you are severely depressed; you have anxiety; you feel a sense of toxic shame; and you have emotional flashbacks that make you feel overwhelmed, helpless, and unworthy. The attacks keep happening day after day, each time getting worse. You realize that you are in an abusive cycle with your partner and confront her about it.

When you stand up to her, she puts the abuse back on you. Every time you point out her behavior, she explodes and twists everything around, saying you are the one abusing her. The situation is one of your making, not hers.

If you feel that you are in an abusive relationship with a person who has NPD, but you are not sure, consider the following signs of Narcissistic Abuse Syndrome and whether any of the scenarios described seem familiar.

Signs of Narcissistic Abuse Syndrome

Detachment and dissociation

In the midst of an episode with your partner, do you feel the need to detach or dissociate yourself from what is happening? If so, this is a sign that something is really going wrong in your relationship. Do you experience a loss of memory or unconsciousness? Do you feel detached from your sense of self?

The problem is that you are going through a situation so terrible that your brain completely removes itself from reality to protect yourself. Such a coping method is unhealthy and fertile ground for substance abuse or other unhealthy activities.

Walking on eggshells

Do you spend your days thinking of preemptive ways to avoid his anger or worry over when or what will make him strike out next? Perhaps you try to stay quiet or to acquiesce to the impossible standards he has set for you. You might be anxious all the time, whether he is with you or not. When you are out in the world without your abuser, do you find that you have lost your ability to be assertive or go through your regular routine?

Do you fall apart when you are around someone who has similar attributes as your abuser?

If you find that you now live your life walking on eggshells and trying not to disturb anyone, or you stop your reactions and hold back your responses because your abuser will get upset and lash out if you do so, then your relationship is unhealthy. There is a way out of this, and we will discuss it in Chapter Seven.

Pleasing the abuser

When you started dating the narcissist, did she want to be a part of your life and meet your friends, coworkers, and family - until she didn't? Maybe she said your friends excluded her, so you stopped seeing them. Your family doesn't like her, so you stop going over for Sunday brunch.

Over time, your main goal became pleasing and satisfying your narcissistic girlfriend. You put aside your desires, wants, and needs to satisfy her's, thinking that doing so would make you content and your relationship peaceful. But the narcissist is never satisfied.

Do not despair; there are many things you can do to get back on track with your life. The first step is to recognize that you are being abused. From there, it gets easier.

Prince Charming

Consider the following scenario:

You were so happy in the beginning. You had initial concerns about jumping too quickly into a relationship but put that worry away and just let it happen. Your narcissist told you that he was special, and only someone similarly special - you - would understand him.

Then, things changed. But after your fights, he made you believe everything would be alright if you just acted the way he wanted you to act. If you just did that, things would go back to the way they were; the two of you could be happy again.

The truth is that you will never be enough for the narcissist. Nothing you do will please him because he can't be pleased. The sooner you realize this, the easier things will be in the end.

Trust issues

During your relationship, the narcissist gaslighted you into believing that your experiences are not valid. Now, you don't know if you can trust your own judgment.

The hardest part is being open to receive friendship or any kind of transaction with another person. Those whom you would have trusted before now put you on edge. You chose the wrong people to let into your life and paid the price. Now, you fear that every person you know will hurt you just as your narcissistic partner has.

This has been the goal of the narcissist. Remember, the first step is realizing what is happening in your life. Be brave, and acknowledge what is happening to you.

Experiencing suicidal thoughts

When was the last time you felt you could just walk out of the traumatic relationship that you are in? Do you dream of walking away, or do you feel that there is no other alternative but to kill yourself or to self-harm in order to cope?

When you engage with your narcissistic partner, the arguments are so traumatic that you can't see any way out but suicide. You begin to dream of killing yourself, and this thought or ideation makes you feel better. In fact, it is those dreams that are keeping you together.

When you do get the courage, he love bombs you and this only serves to confuse you even more. Your world and reality are so twisted, you can't see any normal way of walking away from this relationship, so suicide seems the only way out. It is a fact that victims of intimate partner violence are twice as likely to attempt suicide multiple times. Suicide is the way that narcissistic abuser commits murder without a trace (McKeon, 2014).

If you feel suicidal or have a desire to self-harm, please talk to a licensed professional or a crisis worker for support.

Isolation

Perhaps you realize your relationship is unhealthy. You know the narcissist's behavior is wrong, but feel that you enable him because you are too submissive and weak. You do not want your loved ones to see you in this condition, so you isolate yourself. If so, the narcissist has separated you from your support group - your friends and family.

While there was a time that you would demand boundaries and better treatment from the narcissist, that time has passed. Each time you spoke up, the narcissist would put you down and tell you that you are the reason for the predicament that you are in. Now, it's too late.

If you are in the shadows, it is time for you to come out. There is help available to bring back the self-confident woman you once were.

Self-destruction

Another sign that you are in an unhealthy relationship with a narcissist is when you hear the abuser's voice in your head, and you believe all the negative things he says about you.

Perhaps you once told him your future goals, but he told you that you'd never achieve them. Now, you feel worthless and undeserving of good things; you do not think you have what it takes to do anything (Arabi, 2016).

Remember, the narcissist is covert and ruthless. He will manipulate and tear you down so that he can appear the better person. With proper help, however, you can rebuild your faith in yourself.

Fear

The narcissist hates it when their partner accomplishes a goal that makes them more successful than the narcissist. If your partner punishes you for achieving your goals or steals the credit for your accomplishments, then you likely are in an abusive relationship.

You should not associate success with punishment. Your partner hurts you because she is jealous; she has an inflated sense of superiority, and your actions have challenged that worldview.

Cognitive dissonance

There comes a time in your relationship where you experience a cognitive dissonance because the person that says he loves you treats you so horribly. You cannot rationalize this situation, so you instead minimize what is happening to you. It becomes important that what has happened is no big deal. In fact, you begin to think that you deserved the cruel treatment and that you provoked the narcissist (Arabi, 2016).

It is important that you try to reduce the cognitive dissonance of your partner's words and actions. While reading this book, you can begin to understand the actions of the narcissist. You are not at fault for the way he treats you.

Chapter Summary

- A narcissist will try to isolate you from friends and family
- Being in a relationship with a narcissist is very unhealthy
- It is not your fault that the narcissist is abusive

In the next chapter, you will learn some key traits that a narcissist exhibits.

Chapter Three: How to Spot a Narcissist

It might be difficult to determine if you are in an abusive relationship with a narcissist, but there are several types of behavior that will indicate if you are being abused. In the previous chapter, we discussed some reactions and behaviors you may have if you are in an abusive relationship. In this chapter, we will discuss the abusive narcissist's behavior and some scenarios where it manifests.

The charm offensive

If it seems too good to be true, it probably is. The narcissist, when you first meet, may pursue you single-mindedly. Right from the start, he tells you how special you are and that there isn't anyone like you. He flatters you and calls you rare and unique. He might even say you were brought together by destiny.

The problem with such a man is that eventually, you will do something that disappoints him. It's inevitable because his standards are so high. You won't know what you did to disappoint him, and in fact, there might not even be a real reason for him to be disappointed.

The truth is, there are no shortcuts to a good relationship. The narcissist is moving so quickly because he isn't looking for a partner; he's looking for prey. Once he sees that you are empathetic or sensitive, he knows you will be perfect for the type of relationship he has in mind and will move swiftly to establish that relationship.

Always being right

Nothing spells out narcissist like a person who is never wrong - in her opinion. You may simply see someone with firm convictions who knows what she wants and is decisive in taking it. But the narcissist, more than being firm and taking command, must always be in the right, even when she's not. You point out flaws in her reasoning or times when she's point-blank wrong, and she dismisses everything you have to say.

When you fight, she won't admit to any wrongdoing. She won't even acknowledge that an issue exists. There is no compromise with a narcissist - especially one who doesn't think she had anything to do with the situation. If this situation occurs a single time, there is cause for concern, but there is a larger issue here: not only is she always innocent, but she is also never responsible for what happened.

Eventually, you might lose control because you keep getting upset about something she won't even acknowledge. In such a situation, the narcissist, because she is never at fault, will condescend and suggest that you learn to control your emotions.

When you've finally had enough, walk away without an argument. Don't even waste your breath telling the narcissist anything. She is never wrong, and you are never right.

Too much attention

When you first met the narcissist, he couldn't get enough of you. You had set boundaries and routines, but they didn't matter to him. The narcissist will want all your attention all the time. If you are apart, he will call and text you incessantly. If you ignore your phone, he will try to come at you through social media.

As with other aspects of the narcissist's behavior, he will try and convince you that his ideas and methods are the right ones. Having constant contact is natural if you're with someone as wonderful as him. You should have known that.

The truth, however, is that he doesn't respect your time or your preferences. He doesn't care about your needs. He believes he is entitled to all of your time, not just what you want to allot him. When your "no" seems like a negotiation, this is a red flag (Arabi, 2016).

You do not have to put up with someone being angry at you because you didn't answer a text. There is no need to apologize when you send a call to voicemail. The narcissist is a person who does not respect your right to make your own choices and maintain your boundaries or values (Arabi, 2016).

What relationship?

Imagine the following situation.

You're meeting your partner for dinner at a restaurant. When you step through the door, you look around for your boyfriend, but he isn't at a table; he's at the bar chatting up a woman. You close your eyes and take a deep breath. This can't be him. You take a few steps into the restaurant and squint - this can't be him. And if it is him, she's probably a sister or cousin that he wants you to meet.

You stare at him, hoping that he will see you and wave you over, but when he notices you, he just turns away and gets even closer to the woman. Turning around and leaving seems to be a good option, but you know how furious he would be if you did so. It will be better if you just go to him.

While walking to the bar, you feel the acid churning in your stomach. Eventually, you reach the bar and, with a big smile, place your hand on his shoulder. He turns and looks annoyed. "Hello?" You bend over to give him a kiss as usual, but he turns his face. You can't believe this. It is not like him to do this to you.

The woman looks embarrassed and excuses herself. You feel your face turn flaming red.

If this situation or the man's behavior sounds familiar, it may be because your partner is a textbook narcissist. A narcissist is always on the lookout for someone better, be it a restaurant, a bar, or even an airport. At the same time that he places you on a pedestal, he will treat you as an afterthought. In fact, he likely is constantly looking at other women or smiling over your shoulder. It never stops.

Not all men are like this. The narcissist does not have an excuse for the way he behaves. A person who wants to be with you will not keep checking out the competition for a better option. Even if you are on a casual date, you deserve someone who wants to be in your company.

Sarcasm and the silent treatment

At first, it was playful. It was like the two of you spoke your own language. His sarcasm made you laugh. Until the day it didn't. You weren't expecting that turn of phrase to hurt you, but it does. You think maybe you misunderstood, but your gut tells you that this was no joke.

As time goes on, more and more of his sarcastic comments begin to needle away at you. You speak up, and he denies the whole thing. And then when you won't let it go, he gets angry and doesn't speak to you.

The silent treatment lasts for longer than you expected. When he does start talking to you again, he tells you to change your ways as they are not in line with what he wants for a girlfriend or future mate. He uses provocative words to describe what he wants you to become. He assures you that the change is just for you. Who could stand to be the way you are, after all?

Again, you ask him to tone it down, and again he gives you the silent treatment. He is punishing you for having a thought that is not in line with his thinking or his desires. You can't believe this. He was so kind, sweet, and good-natured in the beginning. What changed him?

It's hard to see something like this coming. Remember that the covert narcissist operates on a stealth level. He is practiced at not being obvious.

Being better than you

The most important thing in any relationship is respect. If you have decided to commit to someone, you are also saying that you love, or at least like, the qualities and attributes that make up that person. You ask them out and spend time with them because you enjoy being with them.

The narcissist does not operate like this. The longer you are together, the less he seems to like you. He calls you names masked as endearments. He makes snide comments that he plays off as jokes. He belittles your achievements in private, and in public, he gives backhanded compliments.

A narcissist cannot stand anyone being better than him. Any good qualities or achievements found in other people must be criticized, so he can inflate his self-worth and maintain his superiority.

Gaslighting

You've spent months holding back because you weren't sure what to do about your relationship with the narcissist. You've made a list of everything unpleasant that the narcissist has said to you, and reason that if he loves you, he will take you seriously and apologize. You are hopeful that this discussion will bring you closer as a couple.

But when you confront him, he turns the tables on you. You may have a list, he says, but he has a book of all the things you do wrong. You mention the sarcasm, the name-calling, the backhanded compliments, and he says you have misunderstood the situation. You're overreacting.

He then proceeds to tell you the things in his book, and these things are almost verbatim what you have said to him. You can't believe it. You try to stay on point and have him acknowledge the things on your list, but he goes into a rage and calls you petty and childish.

This is gaslighting at its best. It's a lose-lose situation. It might seem impossible to you, but most people can handle constructive criticism. A narcissist is not the social norm.

Not feeling good about yourself

These are only a few clinical traits that indicate a red flag when it comes to NPD; however, what really matters is how you feel. Here are some feelings that you might be having:

- You no longer feel like yourself

- You're anxious about everything

- You've lost your self-confidence

- You worry that you've become too sensitive

- You believe that everything you do is wrong

- You feel responsible for everything that goes wrong

- You always say you're sorry

- You feel like something is wrong about your life, but can't pinpoint what it is

- You second guess your reactions to the narcissist

- You make excuses to other people for the narcissist's behavior (Kassel, 2019)

If you feel any of these things, know that there is nothing wrong with you. You are involved with a person who has an ostentatious sense of himself and a need for an unreasonable amount of admiration. It isn't your fault that this person has a preoccupation and fantasy about unlimited success, power, brilliance, beauty, and ideal love (Kassel, 2019).

The narcissist may feel like a monster to you at this point. But he isn't. He is a person just like you or me but one with a corrupted sense of reality. It is possible to break away from his abuse and regain your sanity. We will talk more about this in Chapter Seven.

Chapter Summary
- There are definite ways to spot a narcissist
- A narcissist always believes he is better than you
- A narcissist thrives on making you feel bad about yourself

In the next chapter, you will learn techniques to disarm a narcissist.

Chapter Four: Disarming the Narcissist

Knowing what to say to a narcissist will help you to de-escalate the hostile communication between the two of you. It is possible to focus on what he is saying and take an active part in any heated discussion. You do not have to be a victim. You can be an equal in your conversations with the narcissist.

Below are twenty steps, in no particular order, to help you to disarm the narcissist and have better communication with him or her. Some of these steps may feel contrary to each other. At times, you will feel frustrated and want to walk away from the argument; at other times, you will be able to face the narcissist in a more confident and positive manner. As you gain more control over the situation, you will find it easier to discern when to engage with the narcissist and when to pull back.

Step #1: During a heated discussion with a narcissist, you can alter your communication by using phrases like: "I feel _____ when you say _____."

The narcissist is going to bombard you with confusing statements to put you on the defensive. He wants to turn everything into being your fault. When he throws out a statement that changes the reality of the statement, stop him and tell him that when he says those kinds of things, it makes you feel a certain way. Be specific about the way you feel. He may not care about your feelings, but doing so will make you feel better. It may even turn the tide of the conversation by slowing the narcissist down and making him think about how to regain control of the conversation.

Step #2: You can be an active listener and say things like, "Did I hear you right?" or, "If I understand you correctly, you said . . ." Doing so validates the narcissist and tells him that you are listening to him.

Stay focused and pay attention to what the narcissist is saying. Make the narcissist responsible for everything he says. By having his words repeated back to him, the narcissist will have to clarify statements with facts that he most likely does not have. Do not challenge the narcissist, but calmly ask him to clarify what he is saying to you. As with the first step, these statements will slow down the conversation and show the narcissist that you won't just let him bully you with words.

Step #3: You can take timeouts when you are having heated discussions. Just say, "I'm going to take a short break, and we can continue this later." Make sure to actually take a break after this statement.

When you fight with the narcissist, his goal is to make you unhinged, at which point he will make wild accusations and try to get away with outrageous statements. Stop the momentum that the narcissist is building and walk away. It doesn't make you weak if you do not fight until the end. Stepping back from the conversation will give you a respite from the narcissist's arguments and help you clear your mind. You will definitely come back stronger with some rest and time away from the argument.

Step #4: Detach yourself from feeling like everything is your fault. You are not responsible for what the narcissist is saying or doing. You are not the reason why he behaves the way he does.

In an argument, the narcissist will really hit on the fact that you caused the argument or whatever is going bad in your relationship. If he is having a bad day, anything that happened that day is going to be your fault as well. Don't even think about buying into that argument. Be firm with yourself, and do not believe anything that he is telling you, no matter how much he tries to convince you that you are the reason he is the way he is.

Step #5: Let things go. Let him feel what he wants and do not get involved with it (Arabi, 2016).

Most of the time, there isn't going to be anything you can say to a narcissist to change the course of his attitude or mood. If he's in an agitated state, just let things go. It is alright to be speechless and not have anything to say to the narcissist. This is important, especially when you cannot physically walk away and take a time out. Find a way to stay calm and let the narcissist carry on as usual. It's okay not to have an argument or a defense for what he is trying to put on you. This doesn't make you the loser; it makes you the better person.

Step #6: Don't engage in arguments with the narcissist. Tune him out or walk away when he starts to rant and rave. Don't buy into his arguments.

Make it clear to the narcissist that you are not going to engage in an argument. There will be times when the narcissist argues about things that are important to you. He will make you feel like you must defend your character or the very essence of your being. Know the signs that indicate he is trying to bait you into an argument. Don't fight with the narcissist about inappropriate things that one should not argue about. He doesn't know the difference between a civil conversation and an argument. Be sure that you know that difference and refuse to have anything but a civil conversation at the appropriate times.

Step #7: Keep track of everything: emails, texts, phone messages, even discussions. The more proof you have, the less accusations a narcissist can fling at you. Be armed with the truth when a narcissist gets in your face.

It's a shame that you have to collect evidence, but when you are in a relationship with a narcissist, you need an impenetrable defense. Keep tangible proof at the ready for when he tries to say that you did or didn't do something. There exists a fine line between challenging the narcissist and proving him wrong; your goal is to do the latter by presenting irrefutable evidence that the narcissist cannot dismiss. Learn the art of defending yourself in a civilized manner, and be calm and matter of fact when you produce your evidence.

Step #8: When the narcissist belittles or insults you, blow him off. Don't take him seriously. Understand that the narcissist is demeaning you because he feels insecure. Stop him in his tracks by being confident that you are not the things he is accusing you of being.

Deal and interact with the narcissist from a position of power. Be confident that nothing he says about you is true. Be prepared for the narcissist to pin his inadequacies onto you; become familiar with his usual put-downs and insults. Learn to recognize the strategies he uses to belittle you and know that none of what he is saying is even remotely true. When the narcissist sees that you are neither crumbling nor fighting back, he might just stand down and move on to another subject.

Step #9: Try pouring out compassion and empathy – the narcissist will have to think twice about what he is saying

because you have changed tracks and are connecting with his feelings instead of running from them.

See the narcissist for who he is – a very damaged and sick person. He has a mental illness that he might never be able to understand or admit to having. You are not dealing with a sane or reasonable person. It is not pity that he deserves, but an understanding that things are difficult for him. His world is one where he feels he needs to fight everyone. Disarm the narcissist with kindness.

Step #10: Have confidence and feel good about yourself. Make it known to the narcissist that nothing he says or does is going to bring you down.

Find your own bliss and take this feeling with you wherever you go. Let the narcissist know that nothing he does is going to take you down. Make your world a wonderful place to be in and build lines that the narcissist cannot cross. When you are around the narcissist, be calm and, similarly to in Step #5, do not react when he verbally releases his aggressions. Fortify your emotions and be true to yourself. The narcissist will get the clear message that you are happy, and he won't be able to tear down your happy place.

Step #11: Prepare yourself for what a narcissist might say during an argument or a conversation. Being prepared will take the punch out of his blows.

Your goal is not to prove the narcissist wrong. Your goal is to prevent his arguments from taking you down. If you know to take cover and defend yourself when he starts hurling his put-downs and arguments, the narcissist will not be able to do much real damage. Knowing beforehand that you are not going to succumb to what he says about you will go a long way in protecting you from the foul ideas and thoughts that are going to be thrown your way.

Step #12: Do not react with fear, anger, or impatience. Remain clear-minded as to what the narcissist is telling you. Say things like, "That's interesting. Can you help me with more explanations about that?" or, "Can you please clarify what you said to me?" Doing so will give the narcissist his desired attention while disarming what he is saying (Arabi, 2016).

Acting cool and stoic is not what the narcissist expects from you. He wants dramatic and explosive emotions. As with Steps #1 and #2, if you have deliberate, focused questions about the narcissist's comments, he will have to think twice about what he is saying. When you express interest in what the narcissist is saying, his tactics - false accusations and belittling remarks - are shown to be ineffective. Remember, the narcissist disparages you because doing so elevates his sense of superiority. Feeding into the narcissism by acting interested instead of challenging him is a tricky proposition, but acting in this manner will help you in the long run.

Step #13: Set up emotional boundaries when talking to a narcissist. Don't fall into their trap of wanting to make you feel guilty or responsible for their behavior.

Emotions run high when you are having a discussion with a narcissist. Set up emotional boundaries and stick to them. Teach the narcissist that you will not go to the places that upset you. Start with one boundary and teach it to the narcissist and then go from there building on what you have taught him. Don't challenge him, but make it very evident that you are not going to go to the places that he wants to take you. Be very clear about the boundaries that you intend to keep up in arguments or discussions with the narcissist.

Step#14: Don't let the narcissist control the conversation. Get in there, actively participate in the conversation, and have some impact on the direction the conversation is going.

The narcissist may be an expert at control, but that does not mean that you cannot direct or move the conversation into your corner of the world. When he says something, you do not have to be provocative, but you do need to respond to what he is saying and guide the conversation. Letting the narcissist just say anything he wants is not going to be good for you. Make the narcissist own what he is saying. Pay attention and look for openings in the conversation where you can make a point. You do not have to yell and scream - just stay calm and be an active listener. Ask questions calmly and do not be afraid of the narcissist's answers.

Step #15: Make the narcissist accountable for what he is saying. Ask questions such as "What helped you reach that decision?"; "What things did you consider when making that decision?"; or say, "Help me understand your intent." Use deliberate language and stay focused on what the narcissist is saying.

The narcissist is going to voice slippery thoughts and hurl false accusations at you. He is all about the blame game, and he is very good at it. But you can make the narcissist own what he is saying by being firm and letting him know that you are listening intently to his words. Instead of reacting in anger, ask the narcissist a question about what he is raging about. Break up the narcissist's conversation with thoughtful questions. Respond to what the narcissist is saying by asking him to verify things. He is going to be throwing all kinds of judgment and blame your way – make him back up these theories of his. Have a laser-like focus on all the topics that he is offering up for display. You can sit there and let him whip you with his words, or you can assert yourself into the conversation by letting him know that he isn't going to get away with hostile rhetoric that is designed to hurt you and distract you from what is actually going on.

Step #16: Think pleasant thoughts when you are listening to the narcissist speak. Do not fear him or the conversation. Stay positive, and try to imagine a positive outcome from the conversation (even if there isn't one).

The narcissist trains you to fear him so that he can own the way you feel. The narcissist counts on the process of you becoming emotional and subsequently not hearing what he says. Surprise him by being positive. Think of the fact that he has a mental illness, and that you are not responsible for it. Use that compassion to put yourself at peace with what is going on. He might be blaming you, but that is a symptom of his condition, not the product of anything that you have done. Believe that he cannot hurt you with his words anymore and that when he finishes with whatever he is ranting about, you will do something positive for yourself like make a bubble bath or take a nice peaceful walk.

Step #17: Let the narcissist believe that you are a source of support and recognition instead of someone always ready to fight him.

The narcissist is, in reality, a person lost in his own emotions. When you reach out to the narcissist, take on the role of someone who is compassionate about his situation but not a punching bag to be abused. Be firm and make it clear that while you do not agree with him or what he is trying to make you believe about yourself, you are willing to hear him out. Doing so will stop the narcissist from intensifying his topic and whipping you up in a frenzy of emotion.

Step #18: Adjust your conversation so that you can add positive statements that will change the tone of the conversation. Be sincere in your comments, even though you might be frustrated by what the narcissist is saying.

Saying things like "I'm sorry you feel that way," or "I can see your point" are not going to cost you anything; however, they just might change the tone of the narcissist's speech. Instead of pushing you towards anger, he may calm down just enough to pull back from making his primary goal to hurt you.

Step #19: Always remember that the narcissist can't handle frustration or challenges. Take away his power, and turn these obstacles into opportunities for you and the narcissist.

You do not have to get into the narcissist's face to have an effect on what he is saying. Don't be passive-aggressive either. Just stay calm and focus. Put up your walls, and stay strong. When the narcissist sees that you aren't responding to the blows he is delivering, he will halt his pain-inducing speech.

Step #20: Practice mindfulness every day

By living in the present and not the future, you will be better able to handle the things that are happening to you. If you remain in the present, the past and the future will not overwhelm you. Make it a daily routine to check in with yourself to make sure you are living in the present.

Final Thoughts

Don't argue right off the bat. Let the narcissist say what he needs to before responding in a clearheaded and rational manner.

Set emotional boundaries, and do not let the narcissist cross those lines. Be clear on what you will do if he crosses them – like walking away from the conversation.

Don't be afraid to turn around and leave if you have to.

Be prepared to have the narcissist twist your words around. Be very clear in what you say, and repeat yourself if necessary. Know that the narcissist will accuse you of lying, being unfair, judgmental, or other, worse things. Do not give him the response that he wants when he accuses you of those things. Stay firmly focused on the topic at hand.

In addition to managing your mindset and emotions when interacting with the narcissist, consider taking additional steps to expand your worldview beyond that of the relationship. Having regular interactions with society away from the narcissist's influence will help you see through his potential machinations.

Remove the things that the narcissist will want to use to manipulate you. For example, have your own finances so that he can't manipulate you with money or funds. Maintain a separate cell phone bill or have your own car so the narcissist cannot isolate you from your support network.

Find ways to bolster your self-confidence and self-esteem. Engage with people who encourage you and appreciate your worth. If you have a strong sense of self, the narcissist will not be able to knock you down.

All these things are difficult to do but have confidence that you can do them. Take steps to change control of the situation from the narcissist's hands to yours, no matter how difficult it may seem. You can change your circumstances.

Chapter Summary

- Do not challenge a narcissist because he will become abusive
- Set boundaries that the narcissist can not cross
- Don't be afraid to walk away from a narcissist that is becoming abusive

In the next chapter, you will learn about empaths and narcissists.

Chapter Five: Empaths and Narcissists

What happens when you put a deeply feeling and highly sensitive person in the same room as a narcissist? Well, it's love at first sight. Before the narcissist stands a person who will give him all the understanding and admiration that he so dearly craves. This person, who is thoughtful and caring, sees the charming narcissist as someone who needs a champion, someone who really understands him. The narcissist observes that the empath can be of beneficial use to him, so he warms up to her and sends out a lure that she can't ignore.

What Is an Empath

An empath is someone very sensitive to the emotions around them who feels more strongly than most people. An empath does not have the filters that most people have. While most people can filter out the emotions around them and focus on things at hand, the empath feels everything. Empaths cannot block out stimulation because they have an extremely reactive neurological system (Orloff, 2018). To put succinctly, empaths are "emotional sponges who absorb both the stress and joy of the world" (Orloff, 2018).

While this book will not go in depth into empaths, if you feel you may be empathic or a highly sensitive person, you can learn more on the subject in the other book in this series, "EMPATH AWAKENING," which contains a wealth of information on this subject.

Qualities of the NPD that Attract the Empath

A narcissist spends his life learning how to manipulate people to get his desired results. He develops an attractive demeanor and practices his charisma on everyone he meets. Hence, when an empath meets a narcissist, she can be quite taken with his charm and intelligence. In the beginning, a narcissist is attentive and sweet. When he meets the empath, he is proud of being with her, and his actions and demeanor make the empath acceptive.

This is the beginning of a doomed relationship. The empath will give compassion and understanding to a person who has no heart. Any relationship between the empath and the narcissist will be a toxic one that ends badly – if it is to end at all. The narcissist sees the empath as a person who will fulfill his every desire because their very natures are diametrically opposed. The empath needs to nurture and give herself to something or someone, and the narcissist craves understanding and attention.

The empath basks in the warmth of the narcissist's charm and intelligence, and in the beginning, the narcissist may respond in kind and give back to the empath. But as with others before her, there eventually comes a moment where the empath does something to displease the narcissist, and he responds with coldness. Moreover, the narcissist punishes the empath and withholds the emotions he previously gave effortlessly.

The problem in the relationship does not lie with the empath. It lies with the narcissist who presented a false self. He is not a caring person, nor does he have empathy for others. In fact, he has nothing but contempt for other people, and in this relationship, projects his weaknesses and insecurities on the empath.

A Deceptive Relationship

It is not that the empath is a weak person or a person who is easily deceived. The narcissist, as described in Chapter One, is clever and well-practiced in hiding his true self. The narcissist wants to create chaos and shake things up, and this type of behavior upsets the peace-loving empath. But instead of her instincts telling her to walk away from the relationship as most people would have, the empath feels that her love and devotion can help the narcissist become a better person.

The truth is that the narcissist is never going to change his ways, no matter how much support and devotion the empath gives to him. With his condition, it simply is not possible.

Unhealthy Bonds

The other facet of this relationship is that the more the narcissist abuses the empath, the more she develops a *trauma bond* to the narcissist. What is a trauma bond? A trauma bond is a type of bond between two people in an abusive relationship characterized by ongoing cycles of abuse during which reward and punishment are periodically reinforced. This type of bond is very hard to break.

The empath has no boundaries or filters, so the narcissist takes advantage, systematically castigating and hurling abuse on the empath. The empath, unfortunately, does not realize that not all people are meant to be in her life. The empath does not have the defenses that a regular person would have, and as a result, they are left defenseless to the behavior of the narcissist. Even though the relationship has become painful, the empath believes that she must remain in the relationship, no matter what befalls her. She feels that she can be the person to help the narcissist with some personal growth. The empath begins to concentrate on the potential of the narcissist's behavior instead of on the reality of the narcissist's personality (Dogson, 2018).

Let's examine the narcissist and his negative impact on the empath. Remember that the empath has a uniquely sensitive perception of the world. She believes that the rest of the world is as caring and loving as she is and that she can change the narcissist with her love. But as we already know, a person with NPD has trouble with, or a complete lack of, empathy - he does not understand or is capable of love.

A Narcissist's Behavior

Being a narcissist means that you aren't very concerned with the rest of the world. You choose your companion on the basis that this person can pull you up and take you farther than where you can land on your own. An empath doesn't understand this because she is not the type of person who seeks any kind of status. Both an empath and a narcissist are intuitive, but they use their intuition in different ways. An empath uses her intuition to connect with the people in her life. A narcissist, on the other hand, uses his intuition to manipulate and achieve his goals (Orloff, 2018).

A narcissist can be empathetic, but his empathy does not have anything to do with compassion. It is instead a false quality meant to attract others to him. Remember, the narcissist has a strong desire to be the center of attention. Any, and all, qualities that might potentially attract others are put forth to maximize his chances of admiration and notoriety. When the narcissist is with the empath, he mirrors her compassion and sensitivity without her noticing that he is doing so. The empath, instead of seeing through the narcissist as many people eventually do, falls in love with the narcissist's supposed commonalities and becomes his champion. The narcissist fools her by being smart, funny, and thoughtful in the beginning, but these qualities are all superficial and will fizzle out when the empath tries to take the relationship to a more intimate level.

A Big Target

In a room full of different people, the empath is the biggest and most obvious target for the narcissist. Empaths are targeted by narcissists because narcissists know that they appeal to the good-hearted nature of the empath (Arabi, 2016). Arabi further writes, "Narcissists do not choose us [empaths] because we are like them; they choose us because we are the light to their darkness; regardless of any of our vulnerabilities, we exhibit the gorgeous traits of empathy, compassion, emotional intelligence and authentic confidence that their fragile egotism and false mask could never achieve." (Arabi, 2016).

The empath is sensitive, attentive, innocent, and gullible (Orloff, 2018) - the ideal prey. The empath offers up her whole being to the narcissist, and this is perfect for him. The narcissist needs a fan club president, and the empath is flattered to be offered the position. But as with all relationships with the narcissist, the empath will eventually misstep.

When the narcissist tears into the empath for her perceived mistakes, he will more devastatingly hurt her than if he tore into someone else because the empath has no filters or defenses. The narcissist will adopt his usual strategy for punishment. He will withdraw and become sullen; he will hold back affection. He will deride her every move, blast her with vicious insults, and blame her for everything bad in her life. Any other woman would leave at this point. The empath, however, will not.

The more cruel the narcissist becomes, the more an empath will believe that she can change the narcissist's behavior. She, in her optimistic view, believes the narcissist has the potential to change and become a better person.

But the narcissist will not become a better person. An empath may believe that if a narcissist goes to therapy, everything will change, but the narcissist is not even a suitable candidate for therapy because he never owns his behavior. The narcissist does not understand the concept of taking responsibility for his actions. He only knows how to blame others for his behavior, and if he cannot own his behavior, he can not begin to change it.

There is no accountability in the world of the narcissist. Conflicts happen because other people cause them - that is the main belief of a narcissist. Such a worldview is foreign to the empath, and hence, the relationship between an empath and a narcissist is often an exercise in codependency.

The Codependent Relationship

Codependency is when a person is dependent on another person whom he or she is enabling. Oftentimes, the codependent relationship results in an imbalance of power in which the codependent person enables another person's addiction, mental illness, or underachievement because that other person, in his or her enabled state, validates the codependent person.

Very often, an empath and a narcissist become codependent on each other, a scenario in which the empath becomes the co-narcissist. The narcissist benefits because he has an audience upon which he can validate himself and feel special; the empath accepts the narcissist's injurious behavior and enables his mental illness. The empath also benefits - she feels effective and useful because she is boosting the narcissist's self-esteem and making him "happy."

Unfortunately, because the empath and narcissist have opposing desires and motivations, they cannot both be appeased in this relationship. Whereas an empath does not like conflict and requires peace for her wellbeing, a narcissist likes to cause chaos and trouble to inflate his self-worth. Consequently, the narcissist will create a distressing situation, and the empath, who will avoid conflict at all costs, will not stop him. In the end, the only person who is happy after a chaotic episode is the narcissist himself.

Sometimes, the empath and narcissist are *wound-mates*, a word that means both partners have been hurt or damaged in the same way. For example, if both empath and narcissist had a parental abuser that attacked their self-worth. They will share the pain that was inflicted on them and use this to create a bond between them.

The empath is attracted to the narcissist because he seems to have a high intelligence quotient and is very charismatic. The empath feels that the narcissist is an awesome person who may be able to feel the things that the empath is feeling. A narcissist keeps the relationship he is having with the Empath on a superficial level even though she wants to really connect. The narcissist will pretend intimacy just to satisfy the empath. Overall, the empath is attractive to the narcissist's seductive pull and faux innocence (Arabi, 2016).

If you think you may be in a codependent relationship, you can learn more about this condition in the other book in this series devoted entirely to this subject, entitled, "Am I Codependent? And what do I do about it?" by myself, Kara Lawrence.

The Main Distortion

A narcissist is going to act in the same manner regardless of who he is involved with. He will use always use techniques to degrade and demean that person. It just happens that an empath, with her vulnerabilities, will be the person who is hit hardest by the narcissist behavior. One of the main tools in a narcissist's toolbox is gaslighting. As discussed in other chapters, gaslighting occurs when the narcissist distorts another person's reality or perception. The narcissist sets up a situation with the intention of provoking a reaction, and then he blames the other person for reacting to that situation; he may even suggest they have lost their sanity (Orloff, 2018). As a result, the empath is driven to despair as she questions her rationality.

Moreover, the narcissist will rewrite or deny events that have taken place between him and the empath. The empath is so naïve and without boundaries that she lets the narcissist's truth become hers without question. She may initially try to correct the narcissist but will be met by a wall of cold emotion. If the empath has a concern, the narcissist pays no attention and instead turns it back on her, making the empath feel stupid and foolish for ever being concerned in the first place.

Hope for the Empath

However, it does not have to be a losing situation for an empath if she is with a narcissist. There are strategies that an empath can use to help protect herself. Here are some things that an empath can do:

- Lower her expectations of the narcissist. Stop thinking that the narcissist has an emotional IQ because he does not.

- Stop being manipulated by the narcissist. Start becoming aware of the things a narcissist does to make you do things.

- Understand that a narcissist is a very cool person. There is no amount of emotional support that can make a narcissist to feel.

- If possible, do not fall in love with a narcissist. If you do fall in love, prepare yourself to end the relationship because it is only going to bring you heartache.

- When dealing with the narcissist, stroke his ego. Tell the narcissist how your actions (like leaving him) will benefit him.

Empath and Narcissist – A Terrible Match

Where there is a narcissist, there is sure to be an empath not too far away. These two types of people are unfortunately attracted to each other regardless of the situation because they each have the qualities that the other desires to exploit. The relationship between an empath and a narcissist will never be healthy. Consequently, it is wise for an empath to understand well the characteristics of a narcissist so that she can avoid them. If she does get involved with a narcissist, awareness and protection strategies can help her to stay away from what will undoubtedly become a disastrous relationship.

If you are interested in learning more about this relationship between empath and narcissist specifically, please refer to another book in this series titled "TOXIC MAGNETISM" which is devoted entirely to this topic.

Chapter Summary

- Narcissists are heavily attracted to empaths
- A relationship between an empath and a narcissist is doomed
- Empaths and narcissists often become codependent

In the next chapter, you will learn about mothers who are narcissists.

Chapter Six: Is My Mother a Narcissist?

Just when you think you have everything about your narcissistic relationship figured out, you realize that there is more than one narcissist in your life: your mother, who hides behind the facade of a saint only wanting the very best for her daughter. Remember, a covert narcissist is *covert* for a reason.

It's hard to believe that your mother is a narcissist, but oftentimes, the narcissistic mother is disguised as a long-suffering figure. After all, the very last place someone will look for abuse is with their mother, who, over the years, has unselfishly put up with him or her. Yet, in the case of the covert narcissist mother, she is anything but unselfish.

One of the main traits of a narcissistic mother is that she knows no boundaries. Whereas some mothers will back off and reserve judgment, the narcissistic mother thrives on criticizing her daughter. No topic is off-limits, and when you try to put up some boundaries, you are met with coldness and punishment. This type of mother makes you believe that she is only telling you these things for your own good, because no one else will tell you the things you need to know.

An example of this type of behavior would be the mother criticizing her daughter's wedding dress or venue choice. She will take that wedding and want to make her own mark - her flower choices, her food preferences - on it while disregarding the wants and desires of the bride. You might say that every mother does this, but that is not true. The caring mother is careful with her daughter's feelings. She supports her daughter in demanding situations, instead of making a big fuss.

Abusive Mothering

Since the relationship between a mother and daughter starts at birth, it is unfortunately the case that a daughter will not know any other type of treatment from her mother. You might think it odd to find out your mother has been abusing you when, in reality, your mother has been controlling you and preventing you from developing your own likes and dislikes. Since a narcissistic mother has been controlling all of a daughter's life, the daughter does not know how to protect herself from her mother's abuse. She may appear to be well taken care of physically, but is not so mentally. Moreover, she will not know how to look out for or defend herself from others seeking to manipulate her either.

A narcissistic mother is always at odds with her daughter's choices and behaviors. A narcissistic mother pushes herself and her identity on her daughter to the point where the daughter will not trust her own feelings and impulses (Lancer, 2017). As a result, the daughter ends up relinquishing control and letting her mother decide everything for her. When the day comes that the daughter tries to be independent, she is shot down by her mother's cruel abuse and commentary.

The Toxic Mother's Behavior

Where other mothers give love and support; the narcissistic mother tears down. Where another mother takes pride in her daughter's independence; a narcissistic mother attacks the independence and creates a situation of such selfishness that the daughter's only choice is to sacrifice herself and let her narcissistic mother have her way.

There is nothing good about the narcissistic mother. Every act and utterance is toxic. Yet, the daughter feels that she must love her mother unconditionally, even if the love she receives back is not. The daughter of a toxic and narcissistic mother accommodates her mother's behavior at the cost of losing herself. A daughter's real self is rejected by a narcissistic mother; consequently, the daughter feels ashamed of herself and incapable of doing any good or right thing.

The Elusive Love of a Narcissistic Mother

The daughter of a narcissistic mother lacks the comfort and care that most mothers offer to their daughters. Tenderness is not something that the daughter of a narcissistic mother experiences. Since the covert narcissist thinks highly of herself, the narcissistic mother sees herself as the ideal maternal figure, contrary to reality. She believes that she is perfectly loving and that she excels at raising her daughter. In her eyes, the snide comments and remarks are simply constructive and honest criticisms. After all, if she did not love her daughter, she would not care so much about the daughter's place in the world. The narcissistic mother does not realize that her relationship with her daughter is one of emotional unavailability.

Being at Your Best

The mother with Narcissistic Personality Disorder never thinks that she is doing anything wrong. As a narcissist, she is the center of the universe; her view of the world is obviously the only one worth having. With this mindset, she manipulates her daughter and controls the needs, feelings, and choices that the daughter tries to make on her own (Lancer, 2017).

The mother with NPD cripples her daughter with criticism and control. The daughter must dress and act just like the mother. She must choose hobbies and boyfriends that the NPD mother approves of. The daughter is not a person in her own right but an extension of the NPD mother. If the daughter tries to go out on her own and make her own choices, she is punished severely with criticism and a cold withdrawal of her mother's attention.

At the core of this maternal narcissistic behavior is a mother's envy and expectations of gratitude and compliance (Lancer, 2017). Although the mother appears to be strong, she, as with anyone with NPD, is insecure and void of any true positive self-esteem. Her daughter, consequently, is her unaware rival in this competition to be the best, and, to win, the narcissistic mother undermines her daughter's relationships with friends, siblings, and even her father (Lancer, 2017).

Identifying the Covert Narcissist Mother

It is true that because she is covert, the narcissist mother might be hard to identify, and this fact is aggravated by the fact that the daughter, who would have the most evidence, has never known any other type of behavior. Unfortunately, more often than not, a person only discovers that their parent is a narcissist when they are in therapy or receiving counseling for the very conditions and traits that the parent caused.

However, there are ways outside of analyzing your behavior that can help you identify your mother as a narcissist. If you look back at your childhood or even now in the present day, you will see that there are things your mother says or does to you that are different from the way your spouse's or friends' mothers treat them. Here are some examples that you might find familiar.

The Worthless Daughter and the Perfect Siblings

If you have siblings, you might have been the scapegoat. You might have a brother or a sister that could do no wrong in your mother's eyes, and you were always the flawed child making things difficult for them.

You might have competed with your siblings to gain your mother's approval, and you might remember that trying to please your mother with your behavior never worked. Your brother or sister was always the perfect one that received your mother's praise and attention. But if you discuss with them how you felt growing up, you might be shocked to find that they felt the same competition and lack of approval. In their memories, you were the perfect child! In reality, however, you and your siblings all likely grew up believing that everyone else was better than you and that your inferiority was entirely your own fault because you grew up with a covertly narcissistic parent.

Your Mother Has Two Faces

Growing up with a narcissistic parent can be very confusing because the narcissist has two faces – the public face and the private face. In public, the narcissist mother is the illusion of perfection. She never has a hair out of place, and she prides herself on her perfect mothering skills.

But while she might have shown you off in public, when you got home, she would barrage you with a list of all the things you did wrong that afternoon and possibly back to things from last year. The narcissistic mother has a long memory and will bring up everything she thinks that you have done wrong.

From a clinical perspective, the public persona of the narcissistic mother comes from a place of insecurity and doubt.

Her public face is one of false confidence portrayed by a narcissist who is too shallow to ever analyze her own behavior. Moreover, the public persona is developed because the narcissistic mother's maternal skills are far from adequate, and her self-esteem issues prevent her from making that known.

The Narcissist's Projection

A mother with NPD tries to shape her daughter to be just like herself, but this self is idealized and unrealistic. Instead, the mother with NPD projects onto her daughter many of the traits that she detests in herself. Moreover, the mother may also project perceived traits from her childhood memories of the daughter's maternal grandmother onto the daughter. If you are the daughter, this puts you in an impossible situation, for you are constantly rebuked and chastised for behaviors that you may not even have.

This kind of harsh treatment damages the daughter's self-esteem and makes her insecure and unsure of herself. These insecurities often become dangerous impulses. The daughter, believing herself to be a burden to her mother, may feel that she should not even exist (Lancer, 2018). The daughter does not realize that her mother will never be satisfied with her behavior and will continue to look for validation only to be abused and chastised for her behavior. This type of abuse knows no end and will go on as long as the daughter is unaware that her mother suffers from NPD.

Lasting Effects of the Narcissistic Mother

When a daughter receives so many negative messages from her mother, it is hard for her to grow up feeling strong and confident. Instead, the daughter grows up feeling ashamed and believing that she is unlovable (Lancer, 2018). As a result, the daughter will constantly be on the lookout for approval and more than likely fall into a codependent relationship with yet another narcissist, which perpetuates the cycle of abuse.

The daughter may also have a strong hatred and anger towards her mother that she does not understand. But because self-expression is not something that a narcissistic mother appreciates or fosters, the daughter will see her emotion as yet another clue that she is unlovable and a bad person. She grows to hate herself as well as her mother, and she never makes the connection that her anger comes from abusive and dismissive treatment from her narcissist mother (Lancer, 2017). It takes an outsider or a therapist to evaluate and conclude that the daughter has been abused by a toxic mother with NPD.

If you find that you had this experience growing up, be confident that you can undo the effect of the toxic messages you grew up believing. Not only are there therapies and support groups that can help you erase these messages and replace them with uplifting, affirming ones, but there are steps you can take on your own. The first step to recovery is to be aware and acknowledge that you suffered at the hands of a toxic mother with NPD. Understand that your upbringing, through no fault of your own, explains why you were attracted and fell into a relationship with another person with NPD. You will find that you can change and free yourself from all the negative messages given to you by the narcissistic people in your life.

Chapter Summary

- Women in relationships with narcissistic persons may find that their mothers also suffer from NPD.

- Mother with NPD often project their negative qualities on to their daughters

- Once you realize that your mother has NPD, you can begin recovery.

In the next chapter, you will learn about the importance of going no contact with the narcissist in your life.

Chapter Seven: No Contact

The hardest thing to do in any relationship is to break up. Making the commitment to no longer see a person that you have spent so much intimate time with is very difficult. It means that you need to have the willpower to not reach out to the person when you are feeling weary or incomplete. When you break up with a normal person, the two of you have a mutual agreement to separate and end the relationship. Even if you do contact each other, it will only be platonically. You may, in fact, later be able to see this person and greet each other with kindness and civility.

When you are trying to sever your relationship with a narcissistic person, however, things do not go as smoothly. The narcissist cannot understand that your relationship is over. Even though you are clear on the fact that the relationship is unhealthy and that you want to end things, the narcissist does not understand. He has no concept that the relationship is unhealthy. In fact, things seem great from his perspective. In you, the narcissist has a captivated audience, someone who adores him and makes him feel powerful. In you, the narcissist has an outlet to blame for all his insecurities and negative qualities. If he lets you go, he will have to come to grips with what type of person he truly is. So, he will fight to keep you in this relationship.

What is No Contact

Going no contact is a strategy designed to remove any and all influence the offending party has on your life. In our case, the offending party is the NPD person, and the goal is to reclaim the person you were before the narcissist, reestablish (or develop) your self-esteem, and use time and distance to heal any physical or mental wounds.

When you go no contact with a narcissist, you quite literally should not be in contact. That means moving out, ignoring text messages, and blocking whatever other means the narcissist will try to get your attention. If, however, you still need to be in contact with the narcissist because you have children together or the narcissist is a member of your family, completely cutting off communication will be more difficult or, depending on the situation, impossible. In such a scenario, you will need to find a way to have the least amount of contact possible.

Why Should You Go No Contact

You need to go no contact because you need to spend time away from the negative treatment of the narcissist. You need to heal and become healthy again. You may have developed trauma bonds or codependency with the narcissist; you cannot sever those ties if he is constantly reinforcing them. Remember, the narcissist does not want you to leave, and he will try to *hoover* or triangulate you back into his orbit if you have any contact with him at all.

Understand that you do not have to remain bonded to someone that causes you as much pain as the narcissist does. You owe it to yourself to disconnect from the trauma and find yourself again. Going no contact is the most effective way to do so.

What is Narcissistic Hoovering

The term *hoover* or *hoovering* comes from the brand name of a vacuum cleaner (Hoover). In relation to the actions of a person with NPD, this slang term refers to the fact that the narcissist will try to suck you back into the relationship.

You might think that the reason the narcissist wants to suck you back into the relationship is because he regrets his behavior and want to start over or make amends. But remember that the narcissist is incapable of such nuance. In reality, he wants to *hoover* you back into the relationship so that he can continue to use you as a resource. Specifically, the narcissist wants to be able to get sex, money, and attention whenever he wants. You might even find that the narcissist has a harem of exes that he keeps around in order to fulfill his needs. Remember the worldview of the narcissist and the pedestal he consequently places himself upon - having a harem at his disposal to fulfill his needs is what is most important to him (Arabi, 2018).

The Addiction to Hoovering

Reacting to a narcissist and his attempt to hoover you back into the relationship hits more than your will power. Studies have found that when you are rejected by a love interest, there can be changes in the biochemical attachments that affect brain activity relating to "addiction cravings, rewards, and motivation" (Arabi, 2018). These are the same synaptic structures that are triggered by addictions to substances like cocaine or alcohol.

When you are hoovered by a person who is not good for you, such as the narcissist, there are chemicals in your brain that respond to this relationship, specifically oxytocin, dopamine, cortisol, and serotonin (Arabi, 2018). We will discuss some of these molecules in greater detail in Chapter Nine. Each time you are hoovered, your neurological system becomes more accustomed to the changing molecule concentrations.

Eventually, you will reach a point where you require larger changes more often, generated by the constant push and pull relationship you have with the narcissist. When this happens, you have become addicted to the relationship.

It is important to work with a therapist to get over any addiction you may have for a narcissist. This can be done by not romanticizing the relationship you had with the narcissist. Also, analyzing the abuse that the narcissist did to you can help you to realize how wrong the relationship was for you. It is possible for you to detox from this abusive relationship as long as you view the relationship you had with the narcissist in a realistic way.

The Act of Triangulation

When you break up with a narcissist, he may also try something known as triangulation. This is the process of bringing in another person or group into your relationship to belittle you and make you vie for the narcissist's attention (Arabi, 2018).

You might find yourself in a love triangle with the other members of the narcissist's harem. The narcissist loves to have people fighting for his attention. It boosts his ego and has the added benefit of making you demean yourself. To him, it's a win-win situation. This is the ultimate mind-game for the narcissist.

The narcissist will triangulate in many different ways. He may flirt with other women, or he may carry on a physical or emotional affair while he is in the relationship with you. He may also compare you with other women or make it so that you are too intimidated to confront the other woman about the affair.

When a narcissist pits you against other women, he is devaluing the relationship that he is having with you. When a narcissist used triangulation, he wants to punish you for even thinking about becoming independent of a relationship with him.

The narcissist often uses triangulation after you break up with him. He wants to get your attention and make you regret ever casting him aside. The narcissist hopes that by triangulating you, he can hoover you back into a relationship with him.

Responding to Triangulation

Even though triangulation is a very powerful technique, you can overcome it with some hard work. First, understand and believe that you are irreplaceable. Triangulation hurts because the narcissist would like you to think that you were of no value, that the new person he is involved with can give him the same or more of what you gave him. This is not true. It is important to remember that the narcissist is only trying to create competition.

Another important thing to know is that the narcissist will also abuse the other person. Although it looks like he is treating the other person better than he treated you, this is only an illusion. The beginning of a narcissistic relationship is always fanciful, but that condition is short-lived.

It is very important that you rebuild your self-confidence so that you can withstand the temptation to compare yourself to the other person that the narcissist has a relationship with. Just because the narcissist is using another woman to trigger you does not mean that she is better than you. She is just a tool that the narcissist is using against you.

You must target the things the narcissist is trying to wound you with and fight back with a new sense of self-worth. You may need to go to therapy in order to relearn the things that are good about you. Surround yourself with people who know your true value.

Overall, you need to put time into yourself for yourself. You might be tempted to go back to the narcissist so that you will feel whole again. But, remember that although you felt a certain level of security in the relationship, it was abusive and not good for you.

Do not fall for the competition or succumb to the jealousy that the narcissist is trying to trigger. Have confidence in the decision you made to end your relationship with the narcissist.

How the Narcissist Will React

When you first cut off the narcissist, the narcissist will panic and try anything to get you back. He will pursue you with a vengeance. He will beg you, promise to change, and make all sorts of promises - anything to keep you. He knows exactly what you want, and he will have no problem using this information to try and manipulate you.

He will be at all the places you habitually go to. The narcissist may stalk your workplace, and he will try to call and text you at any given opportunity. He will blow up social media in a way you never knew possible. There will be endless emails that either curse you or praise you, depending on the narcissist's frame of mind.

When the narcissist realizes that you are not coming back, he will quickly shift his tone. He will slander you and tell anyone who will listen that you didn't deserve him. In fact, the narcissist will spread the word that he dumped you and not the other way around. He may send hurtful, demeaning messages. In the narcissist's mind, he is the wronged party. In his worldview, no one would ever want to leave him, so when you do so, you disrupt his sense of reality. Hence, you need to be punished to put things back in order. When he sees your friends, he will make sure to be with someone that will make you feel inadequate. The narcissist will put out the word that this person is way better than you ever were (Kassel, 2019).

Things the narcissist will do to get you back:

- He will stalk you for an opportunity to talk to you.
- He will call and text you at all hours.
- He will be all over your social media.
- He will send emails that plead with you to get back with him.
- He will show up at your work and embarrass you.
- He will contact your friends and relatives.

You need to prepare yourself for when the narcissist tries to manipulate you. He or she will give you gifts, promises, and tears. They will become your favorite romantic character to get you back. He or she will try to convince you that you were happy together and that you were the perfect couple ("Narcissists and the No Contact Rule").

Things to Do When You Go No Contact

Going no contact is not a healing method. It is the beginning step that will lead you to healing, but more work has to be done before you recover from the unhealthy relationship you had with a narcissist. As stated earlier, the narcissist does not want you to go away and will do everything in his power to keep you close, so it is up to you to stay away.

Here are some recommended things you can do to establish no contact:

- No more meeting the narcissist, whether privately or publicly. Just do not give him the chance to talk you out of ending the relationship.

- Don't talk on the phone with the narcissist. The narcissist is not capable of having a healthy conversation.

- Block all text messages or contact through social media. Be brave, and don't cyber-stalk the narcissist. It is not healthy to monitor the narcissist, and in fact, it could be dangerous. Specifically, he will use every opportunity to entice you to come back to him. He will try to make you jealous and turn the tide by looking like he is making new friends and leading a happy life without you. This is going to hurt, so do not even think of causing yourself more pain by keeping track of what is going on in his or her life.

- Get off of social media so that the narcissist can't find you. If he sees that you are hanging out with certain people or going to public places, he will find a way to meet-up with you. Don't provide a map and a program for the narcissist.

- Remember that going no contact is not a way to improve your relationship with the narcissist. This is the end, not a tactic to make the narcissist change.

- If you have common friends, have no contact with them because you can't take a chance that the narcissist will meet up with you through them.

Establish and stick to your boundaries

There are places and people that you will not be able to avoid. The narcissist will most likely know your home and work addresses, and he may wait for you at these places. You need to be firm about the boundaries that you set. If the narcissist shows up at work, ask for security to take him away. This will show the narcissist that there are outside, societal consequences to his actions, and he may think twice before visiting again. If he still does not realize seeing you at work is off-limits, stand your ground and do not make any exceptions. No contact means no contact. If you need to get help, do not hesitate to get it. If you think you need a restraining order, ask a lawyer to help you get one. Doing these things might just keep you safe.

Get rid of triggers

Seeing pictures or emails of the narcissist can trigger you, so get rid of as many of them as you can. Take down the pictures or delete them from your computer. Get rid of any gifts the narcissist gave you or any other physical reminders of your relationship. Going no contact is very difficult, and you will have moments where you will be tempted to go back. If you have triggers around you, they could bring you right back into the narcissist's arms. Be mindful of the things or places that trigger you, and get rid of things and avoid places that upset you.

The next step is not to go to any place that the narcissist frequents. These are the first places the narcissist is going to go once you initiate no contact. You have gone to all these steps to remove him from your life, so why go somewhere where you know you will see him? The narcissist has made your life very unhealthy; consequently, you need to get rid of him so that you can begin to heal. By establishing no contact, you will ensure your safety and well-being.

Maintain a healthy support circle

There will be demanding times ahead. It is very hard to avoid a narcissist when he is pushing himself into your life. He is going to conduct a smear campaign and try to turn friends and relatives against you. Remember that these people may not know him as well as you do. They will only know the false face that the narcissist puts forth, which is charming and charismatic. In fact, there will be people who do not understand your need for no contact. To them, the narcissist is not capable of abuse.

Do not waste your time trying to convince these people that the narcissist is abusive. In time, the narcissist's true self will emerge. And, if it doesn't, consider removing his fan club from your life. Find new sources of support. Yes, it is hard to find new friends, but you need people in your life who will trust and support your decisions, not people who will try to undermine them. Your priority is to recover from your relationship; you should not have to invest energy in constantly defending yourself.

Keep busy

There are things you can do to make no contact successful. You can change your life by filling up your schedule with things that you like to do. You can try going to a gym or joining a yoga class. You can take some classes at your local college. Do anything that keeps you busy. Seek out new relationships and friendships. This is the time to establish new support networks. Not only should you be filling your life up with more activities, you should also be taking care of yourself. Try getting enough sleep. Eat healthy meals and exercise regularly.

Live in the moment and appreciate your new life. This is not the time to be dwelling on the past. Consider therapy or counseling. Seek out people and situations that teach you new life skills. There is no limit to the things you can do to heal yourself. No contact is the beginning and not the end of what you need to start doing for yourself.

The hardest thing about no contact is that you will be trying to get rid of your addiction to an unhealthy relationship. You might feel that you need to take revenge against the narcissist. It is natural to have a lot of anger about what has happened to you but try to keep these feelings in check. If you can't do this on your own, seek the help you need to get rid of these toxic feelings. Remember that no contact is the gateway to healing.

There will be times when you fall back on your efforts to establish no contact. You might succumb to the narcissist's campaign to get you back. But remember that a narcissist cannot change his behavior because he does not understand that he did anything wrong in the first place. If you go back, at some point, the narcissist will abuse you again.

If you do find yourself with the narcissist again, do not feel that just because you did not succeed with no contact previously, you cannot do so in the future. It is possible to learn from your mistakes and succeed the second, third, or even fourth time around.

Preemptive Steps to Going No Contact

Although you might be in a place where you need to establish no contact right away, it is good to prepare beforehand. If you can do these things before you go no contact, you will have a better chance of succeeding.

- Remind yourself that you deserve a better relationship

- Chose to be around friends that are empathetic to your relationship

- Build a support network that will be there for you during tough times

- Urge the narcissist to go to therapy

- Find a therapist that is an expert on Narcissistic Personality Disorder (Kassel, 2019)

What to Do If You Cannot Go No Contact

When you have a family member who is a narcissist, it is almost impossible to go no contact. However, there are still some things you can do to separate yourself from the narcissist, even if she must remain in your life.

Bring contact with the narcissist to a minimum

There will be times where your children have to see their other parent or their grandparents. Be firm about not talking to her when she arrives to pick up the children. Even better, ask someone to drop your children off at her place so you do not have to see her. If such aid is not possible, seek a neutral place where she will not get the opportunity to start a fight.

Establish strong boundaries

Do not let the narcissist get into your head. Make your home a safe place where she no longer exists. If she comes to your door begging to see you, or worse, wanting to tell you off, get rid of him. Your home is your safe place, and she does not belong there. Do the same thing with your workplace. Designate these places to be areas that your narcissist can not access.

Keep your children safe and healthy

Educate your children about their narcissistic parent in appropriate ways. This is not the time to talk her down or rage about her behavior, but explain in an age-appropriate level that the narcissist is sick and unable to express herself in other ways. Discuss the children's visit with the narcissist, and try to undo any damage she has tried to do. If the children are very upset, consider family therapy as a way to keep the children healthy despite the narcissist's efforts to do the opposite.

Be calm and non-emotional

If you have to see the narcissist, do not let her get to you. Be calm and do not react to what she says. The narcissist is going to use everything she can to set you back. Remember, she thrives on your reactions - they validate her. She will not be happy that you are doing well without her. Ignore the things she is telling you and find your place of bliss after dealing with the narcissist.

Limit telephone time and texting with your children

Do not give the narcissist a chance to get to you through your children. If they talk to her on the phone, have a time limit for the conversation and cut it short if the child becomes upset. Also, put a limit on texting and monitor the texts that the narcissist is sending to the children. If the children are getting very upset, perhaps it is time to contact a family lawyer to set up so permanent boundaries.

Instruct your children about coping skills

You are your children's example as to how to behave with a narcissist. Don't be afraid to role play with your children so that they can learn the best way to deal with their narcissistic relative. You do not have to demonize the narcissist to your children, but you can make them aware of behaviors that are not healthy. Help your children to develop coping skills for dealing with their narcissistic parent.

Do not criticize or complain about the narcissist in front of your children

There is a fine line between educating your children and criticizing the narcissist. Be very careful not to make the narcissistic relative look like a monster. Instead, consider bolstering the narcissist's image by talking with your children about his or her positive traits. Keep the balance in front of your children. Remember, this is their family member, and it is good for them to have a positive outlook on this relative.

Understand that there is no cure for the narcissist

Be realistic about dealing with the narcissist. There will not be a time when you can co-parent. Unless he or she goes to a therapist, they will remain unhealthy for you to deal with. Do not loosen boundaries or stop monitoring your children as time passes. Remember that no contact is the healthiest way for you to deal with the narcissist. If possible, take your children and yourself to family therapy, so that you can learn techniques to deal with the narcissist parent in your life (Esposito, 2015).

After Going No Contact

As you go about establishing no contact, you may feel that you will never be at a point where the narcissist is out of your head. Start the process of getting him out of your head by being mindful and dealing with the present. Don't get overwhelmed by thinking of your past or the future without the narcissist. Be careful about your emotions, and do not get into any drama the narcissist will try to create.

The big picture is that your life is about to get a lot easier. In the beginning, the narcissist will fight to get you back; he will, however, give up eventually, either when he understands and moves on or, if need be, when law enforcement steps in. In either case, when he gives up, you will not have to fight so hard to remain in the no contact zone.

When you are going through the worst of it, create safe places for yourself. Perhaps there is a library where you can go to find some peace. Even the local coffee house or Starbucks can become a safe place where you can relax and think of other things.

If you have children, remain committed to keeping them safe and healthy. When the narcissist blows hot with his tactics and comments, you blow cold. Don't get into a fight over the narcissist's actions because this is what he wants you to do (Esposito, 2019).

Be confident about going no contact. It isn't an impossible thing to do. Ask for help and support to get you through this challenging time. You will find strength that you never knew you had. Trust yourself that no contact is the right thing to do in your situation.

Chapter Summary

- No contact means not seeing the narcissist anymore
- No contact is the healthy choice for a new beginning
- A narcissist will try anything to get back in touch with you
- Stay strong and do not be afraid to ask for help when you go no contact
- There are strategies you can use if you have to see the narcissist.

In the next chapter, you will learn the different types of therapies that can help you cope and begin healing.

Chapter Eight: Beginning Recovery

By this chapter, you likely realize that having a relationship with a covert narcissist can be very damaging to your psyche. You have endured emotional abuse to the point that you need to plan a recovery. Any length of time that you are exposed to this kind of behavior may lead to emotional trauma, an anxiety disorder, depression, or post-traumatic stress (PTSD). Moreover, you will experience a change in your otherwise normal behavior. This is nothing to be ashamed of. You did not do any of this on purpose. You gave yourself whole-heartedly to a person without realizing that they would harm you.

Do not despair; there is something that you can do about this. You can receive therapy in order to alleviate the symptoms of your abuse. There are many different types of therapy, and we will explore some of them to see which one suits you the best.

Again, it is important to remember that you did not do this to yourself on purpose. You engaged in a relationship that you thought would be beneficial to you. The covert narcissist tricked you into believing that he was a whole person, capable of being in a loving relationship.

Starting Therapy

Going into therapy can be very challenging, but when you end your relationship with the covert narcissist, it is not uncommon to have doubts or second-guess your actions. You may feel conflicted. Part of you understands that the relationship is over; the narcissist is dangerous, and you need to get far away from this person. The other part, however, misses the narcissist. Not every second was difficult; there were good times as well.

Therapy can help you work through your relationship. It can help you realize that you, as many often do, remember the good parts of the relationship and suppress the bad parts.

When you start therapy, you have to ask yourself questions about the abuse. The questions and answers you have will help you to understand the relationship that you had with the narcissist. It is important that you find a trained professional and answer these questions in a therapeutic environment. It is important for you to feel safe, and the right therapist or counselor is trained to guide you through these questions with as little trauma as possible (Fritscher, 2018).

Below are some potential questions to consider:

- When did the abuse start?

- How long did the abuse happen?

- How did the abuse make you feel?

- Did you try to tell your abuser that he was hurting you? What was his or her response?

- Did your abuser ever get violent with you? If so, how did the violence start?

- How often did the violence occur?

- What began the abusive treatment?

- What happens after an abusive treatment?

In whatever type of therapy you choose, you will discover the different traits of your abuser and how he hurt you. You will learn that there was nothing you could have done to change his behavior. If you have lingering doubts that your narcissist will find a better person than you, remember that he or she has a long history of hurting people. It is important that you internalize that you are not at fault for any abusive behavior suffered from the narcissist.

With a therapist to guide you, uncovering the cruel treatment of a narcissist can be a very healing process. Below are some further questions to consider when coming to terms with your abuse and trying to move on from it.

Questions to Reflect Upon

1. What are the thoughts about your relationship holding you back? Write them down.

The answers to this question can range from *the treatment I received was my own fault* to *I will never find someone that loves me better*. It is hard to differentiate your feelings in your heart from the facts in your mind. While your mind knows that the way you were treated was very wrong, your heart is telling you a different story. In fact, your heart may be begging you to return to the narcissist to stop the heartbreak. The back and forth arguing between your mind and your heart can get crazy, so consider writing in a journal to make sense of your thoughts.

2. Were you ever treated this way before?

If you can establish that there have been other narcissists or abusers in your life, it might make it easier to understand why you were in a relationship with a narcissist in the first place. Was this the first time that you have ever been abused in a relationship, or are such relationships habitual? The more you can understand your history, the easier it will be to start working on any self-blame or shame that you have. It is important to isolate the negative things that you have been told when you were in inappropriate relationships because it may have been these false beliefs about yourself that led you into the abusive relationship in the first place. A well-trained therapist can help you to explore these thoughts and replace them with positive statements that will help you heal.

3. Do you blame yourself for the way you have been treated?

One of the key behaviors of the narcissist was to blame you for the negative way he treated you. Even when you would call him out on his abusive behavior, he twisted the situation around until you were the instigator and reason for discord in the relationship. After a while, and after many more of these negative occurrences, you began to believe that, indeed, it was your fault. Write down these false accusations, and understand that you had nothing to do with the narcissist's injurious behavior. Realize that you were with a frightened and insecure person who was not ready and arguably unable to own his behavior.

4. Recall the various stages of your relationship and begin to understand the separate phases of the narcissistic abuse.

In the beginning, the narcissist was on his best behavior. It was important for him or her to charm you and to entice you into falling in love with him or her. You felt that you had met the perfect person to fall in love with. Then, your relationship started having difficulties. How did he transform from a loving partner to a manipulative abuser? When in your relationship did it occur? What was the catalyst, if any?

If you can trace back to when the abuse started, you can start to understand what was not true. You will see when his charismatic facade began to crack, and his true nature came out, and you will see that it coincided with the time in which he began tearing you down. The narcissist's maltreatment started small and then built up to whole-scale abusive scenarios. Remember the person that you were before the abuse started and begin to understand the falseness of the narcissistic person's claims about you.

Your Therapy Options

Unfortunately, many people coming out of abusive relationships will have marked emotional trauma. During your relationship, the narcissist degraded and belittled you with derogatory words and actions to the point where the psychological abuse left you with anxiety or a host of other mental struggles. Depression, in particular, is a common symptom of abuse. From here to the end of the chapter, we will discuss specific therapeutic methods to help you with your depression.

To start with, a therapist may suggest psychotherapy, which is sometimes called talk therapy. In talk therapy, you will be alone with a therapist, and he or she will engage you in a variety of techniques that aim to help you uncover the thoughts and feelings that are doing you harm. Furthermore, talk therapy will help you to learn different techniques for coping with your depression.

Let's explore the types of therapies that a licensed professional will guide you through.

Cognitive therapy

Cognitive therapy was developed in the 1960s by Dr. Aaron T. Beck, a psychiatrist at the University of Pennsylvania, specifically to help work on a patient's depression.

Dr. Beck found that people have unconscious and automatic thoughts that are sometimes negative and proposed that it is these negative thoughts that are harmful. Dr. Beck helped his patients identify, evaluate, and train their unconscious thoughts to think more realistically. When patients did this, they were able to feel better emotionally and function better. In particular, when a patient was able to change their beliefs about themselves, they were able to experience long-lasting change.

Today, at the center of modern cognitive therapy is the belief that our thoughts affect our emotions. If we have negative thoughts, we will experience negative emotions. If we have positive thoughts, we will have positive emotions. Of course, it is not necessarily that simple to accomplish or control our emotions. As human beings, we have a complex mix of thoughts and beliefs that cannot simply be categorized as good or bad. Therefore, our behavior has many layers that need to be examined.

Cognitive therapy is short-term and goal-focused. Each session is very structured, and you will have homework to do between therapy sessions. You can expect for cognitive therapy to last between 6 to 18 weeks (Schimmelpfennig, 2019).

This type of therapy will help you examine the automatic thoughts that you are having about your relationship with a narcissist. You will be able to distinguish between the beliefs that the narcissist forced onto you and the reality of who you are. Correcting the automatic thoughts that you have developed in your relationship with a narcissist will help you to erase the thoughts that the narcissist help build.

Behavioral therapy

Another type of therapy that you might want to consider is behavioral therapy. This is a type of therapy that focuses on the undesirable behaviors that you will want to change. It uses the principles of classical and operant conditioning to reinforce desirable behaviors and get rid of unwanted or maladaptive behaviors (Cherry, 2019).

Behavioral therapy uses techniques such as aversion therapy and systemic desensitization to accomplish its objectives. Aversion therapy is when unhealthy behaviors are paired with negative outcomes. For example, if you overeat as a way to cope with your negative feelings, you will learn to pair this overconsumption with feelings of illness. Then, you will stop doing this type of behavior in order to cope. Systemic desensitization happens when feelings of sadness are paired with relaxation techniques. The purpose of doing this is for you to change your behavior. In other words, through systemic desensitization, where you once felt pain and sadness, you will now feel calm and relaxed.

Behavioral therapy is very action-based; therefore, a behavioral therapist is going to focus on learning strategies that will help you get rid of unwanted behaviors. Therapists who use behavioral therapy believe that the behavior is the problem; teaching new behaviors will eliminate the issue. Specifically, old learning led to the problem in the first place, so new learning will fix it (Cherry, 2019).

There are three different behavioral techniques that are used in behavior therapy, and these are cognitive-behavioral therapy, applied behavior analysis, and social learning theory. In all three, you will learn to isolate the behavior that is causing your troubles and replace it with new behavior that alleviates your symptoms.

Cognitive-behavioral therapy

Cognitive therapy and behavioral therapy are often combined to help treat depression and anxiety disorders. When they are combined, the resulting therapy is called cognitive-behavioral therapy (CBT). An example of this type of therapy could be a situation like the following: Your therapist has you write in a journal all the events that happen to you in a week. She will then have you identify the self-defeating and negative reactions to those events. When you do this task, your therapist will be able to teach you new ways of thinking and responding to these kinds of events. You will also learn to practice positive self-talk (Schimelpfening, 2019).

CBT therapy is brief and very goal oriented. It involves between 5 to 30 sessions focused on addressing specific concerns. This type of therapy can be very helpful in teaching you to unlearn all the negative behavior that you learned during your relationship with a narcissist.

Dialectical behavior therapy

Dialectical behavior therapy (DBT) is very similar to CBT because its main purpose is to teach people how to deal with stress, regulate their emotions, and improve their relationships with others (Schimelpfening, 2019). This type of therapy deals with the philosophical process known as dialectics. Dialectics is a concept that everything is composed of opposites. Change occurs when one opposing force is stronger than another.

Dialectical behavior therapy will often use the traditional Buddhist concept of mindfulness. Mindfulness is when you are fully aware of the present moment without judgment. When you are being mindful, you are not thinking about the past, nor are you projecting into your future; you are just in the present - the now.

In order to become mindful, you slow down and become aware of your breath and the sensations in your body. Doing this really helps to make you more aware of what is going on inside of you. The beauty of mindfulness is that you do not have to believe in Eastern philosophies for it to be effective.

DBT has proven to be very effective in the treatment of depression. By helping you to be mindful, you will be able to not be mired in your past or worry incessantly about your future. This can be very useful when you are coming out of a relationship with a narcissist. By being mindful, you can erase all the negative thoughts that were put in your head by the narcissist.

Another helpful reason to consider DBT is that your therapist will be available for crisis coaching and can guide you through demanding situations. Your therapist becomes your teacher, and he or she teaches you how to cope through crisis in more effective ways, including how to get through the no contact phase of separating from your abuser.

Interpersonal therapy

Enduring a relationship with a narcissist can trigger conflict that develops into full-blown depression. Interpersonal therapy focuses on your past and present social roles and interpersonal interactions (Schimelpfening, 2019). It examines your relationships with the narcissist and other important people in your life. The goal of looking into your relationships is for you to identify how these relationships play out in your life. In doing so, you will be able to resolve your relationship with the narcissist, and perhaps undo some of the behaviors that you acquired during your relationship.

Your therapist will ask you to role-play different situations so that you can practice and improve your methods of communication with the people in your life. For example, you can practice how you will deal with the narcissist in your life. You will also be asked to produce strategies that will help you to build a stronger support system.

This type of therapy deals more with the present than it does the past, which can be very helpful because it is in the present that you need most of your help. Dealing with the narcissist can play havoc with your present life. Trying to go no contact while getting over your relationship can be very difficult. Interpersonal Therapy can help you to come up with strategies for coping with the difficult situations in your life.

Different Therapy Formats

When we think of therapy, we mostly think of individual therapy. This is where the therapist works with a patient one-on-one. When you are in individual therapy, you get the full attention of a therapist, and you focus primarily on your own behaviors and ways to change the negative ones affecting your life. However, there are different formats for therapy, including family, group, or couples therapy.

As the name suggests, family therapy is when you go to therapy with your family so that you can work on the dynamics within this group (Schimelpfening, 2019). This type of therapy can be very helpful if the narcissist in your life was part of your family because the other members of your family will also be going through issues resulting from their relationship with the narcissist. In a family therapy, you can all work towards learning new strategies to cope.

Group therapy is a format where you see a therapist with a group ranging from three to fifteen people. This type of therapy can be good for you if you want the support of a group while you are working through issues, and some people prefer this type of therapy because there is less pressure on the individual. There are many different types of group therapy focusing on a range of different issues, including those for survivors of narcissistic or abusive relationships. You can learn from the experiences and healing processes of others while you are in group therapy.

Couples therapy is also a format that you might consider if your relationship with the narcissist is something you cannot get out of. Some people cannot afford to get divorced or have religious reasons that stop them from divorcing. This type of therapy can help a couple function better.

Choosing which therapy format to follow is up to you. You are uniquely qualified to choose the format best suited for your personality, needs, and situation.

The Issues You Are Left to Deal With

Your relationship with a narcissist may have left you with some pretty profound issues, but there are various ways to cope with these issues and learn from them. Knowing what types of therapies are available can help you to choose an effective therapist that will help you to get stronger and resolve the unhealthy issues that you have developed.

Many therapists are learned in more than one specific counseling format. Interview your therapist to learn which types of therapy are their strengths. Choosing the right therapist can really have a significant impact on the way you heal from your relationship with a narcissist, so do not be afraid to interview your therapist before you sign on. Schedule as many information sessions with different therapists as possible before you make the decision to work with one. You might feel overwhelmed and just want to go with the first therapist on your list, but making sure your therapist is the right fit for you is crucial to your success. Just remember that you are capable of doing things that are good for you.

Chapter Summary

- It is important to realize that you may need help to heal from your narcissistic relationship

- There are many different types of therapy that can help you

- Make an effort to find the best therapist for your needs

In the next chapter, you will learn alternatives to traditional clinical therapy.

Chapter Nine: Alternative Therapies

Healing from a relationship with a narcissist can be an arduous process. When you are in a relationship with a covert narcissist, you begin to lose track of who you are. So often, the covert narcissist takes the things that we identify ourselves with and twists them into something that we are not. It can be hard to untangle from these very painful moments.

Therapy is a way to heal ourselves from the cruel treatment we have received from the narcissist. No contact is the beginning of our healing. Mainstream therapies are very good for explaining what has happened and helping you become stronger after the relationship ends. But at times, you might need additional therapy or decide that an alternative method might be better for you. In this chapter, we will examine alternative therapies that you can pursue to begin your healing.

Alternative Therapies

Choosing to use alternative therapy may really benefit you, and you can use alternative healing methods in conjunction with traditional counseling as methods such as yoga, herbal remedies, and guided imagery can easily be integrated into other therapeutic healing techniques ("Depression", 2019).

They can make mainstream therapy more effective as well. For example, your therapist might want to use hypnosis or aromatherapy in order to calm you so that you can venture further into your therapy. It is not unusual for the process of psychotherapy to be difficult. Having something that can help you to get through the difficulty can be very beneficial to your overall progress.

Let's explore the various kinds of integrative therapies so that you can know and understand the alternatives that are out there for you.

Herbal therapy

Herbal therapy can be something that you can use to help manage the symptoms of your anxiety and depression. The main difference between prescription drugs and herbal remedies is that the FDA strictly regulates prescription medication but not plant products ("Herbal", 2019). For your safety, however, consult an expert before ingesting anything unknown. We can be tempted to do our checks on our own, but it is hard to predict how your body will take to different herbs. It is important for a practitioner to run tests and take a full medical history to look for any potential biochemical reasons behind your depression symptoms. Your practitioner may check for substances like Vitamin D and folate to get a better understanding of any hormone or nutritional imbalances that you may have ("Depression", 2019).

Once you have the all-clear, there are many different herbs that your practitioner can use. When it comes to depression, however, the most reached-for herbs are St. John's wort and ginkgo biloba.

St. John's wort

St. John's wort, or *Hypericum perforatum*, has been in use for over a thousand years. It has not been scientifically proven to treat depression, but it is commonly used in herbal therapy. St. John's Caution should be exercised when using St. John's wort if on medication, however, because it may potentially interfere with antidepressants.

Ginkgo biloba

Ginkgo biloba, also known simply as ginkgo or maidenhair, is another plant commonly given to improve memory and focus. To date, ginkgo biloba has not been tested fully, but it has been used for many years to treat depression.

Ginseng

Preferably, source ginseng from America or Asia. Ginseng from other parts of the world are not the same. This herb has been used by the Chinese for over a thousand years to improve energy, clear the mind, and reduce stress (Galan, 2018). Ginseng is recommended to people suffering depression because it may help boost a depressed person's low-energy and motivation.

Chamomile

Although further studies are necessary, chamomile was shown to be effective in managing depression and anxiety over a placebo. Further testing needs to be done to confirm these effects.

Lavender

Lavender is an essential oil that is taken for its ability to lower stress and anxiety. Lavender has also been thought to help improve sleep.

Saffron

This herb has been known to control the symptoms of depression.

SAMe (S-adenosyl methione)

A synthetic form of a naturally occurring chemical in the body, SAMe has achieved significant results when used to treat depression compared to a placebo. It also had an equal effect to the antidepressants imipramine or escitalopram.

While SAMe is used as a prescription antidepressant in Europe, it has not yet been approved for use in the US.

Omega-3 fatty acids

Although not approved for depression, Omega-3 fatty acids can be taken when a person has a deficiency as it helps improve brain function in general.

5-HTP (5-hydroxytrptophan)

A supplement useful for regulating levels of serotonin, 5-HTP is sold over the counter in the US but may require a prescription in other countries. 5-HTP should not be taken in excess because it has the potential to cause a serious neurological complication (Galan, 2019).

Forms of Herbal Supplements

There are many different forms of herbal supplements, including dried, chopped, powdered, capsule, or liquid. As such, they can be applied in a myriad of ways, such as swallowed as pills, powders, or tinctures; brewed as tea; or applied to the skin as a gel, lotion, or cream. You can also add some herbal supplements into your bath.

Herbal therapy, though unregulated, has thousands of years of anecdotal evidence. Hence, you might feel that it is unnecessary to contact a doctor before using these supplements because they have gone through the test of time. Still, always source high-quality herbal supplements and consult your doctor ahead of time so that he can determine if they will interact badly with any medications that you are currently taking.

Acupuncture

Acupuncture is an ancient Chinese method for healing the body from various ailments. If you are suffering from depression or anxiety due to your relationship with a narcissist, acupuncture might help to relieve some of the symptoms that you are having.

In this alternative therapy, very fine needles are placed at specific points of your body. The placement of the needles helps to stimulate your body's ability to correct imbalances that may be occurring. Acupuncture also helps the body decrease or eliminate painful sensations ("Depression", 2019).

There is a recent clinical study that shows acupuncture is effective in decreasing depression within a three-month period. As depression often has physical symptoms such as different aches and pains, acupuncture can help relieve some of the physical pain that you are having due to depression.

Exercise

Although the last thing you want to do when you are depressed or anxious is exercise, doing so can be the very thing that speeds your recovery. Dealing with the abrupt, negative changes that can arise from your relationship with a narcissist can be very stressful and energy-zapping. It is good to get your blood flowing with some exercise as a form of distraction from these issues.

One of the most powerful symptoms of depression is the urge to sleep continuously. Sleeping away your problems may seem the easy solution, but you will have to deal with your emotions eventually. Getting active can help to soothe your nerves and give you energy to do the things you need to do.

Exercise may not be the obvious cure, but it can help release important hormones that can help soothe you and make dealing with depression easier. A vigorous walk in the morning or a calm walk in the evening can really make a difference in your mood.

Doing exercises like aerobics can help you to get rid of some of the nervous energy that is built up inside of you. Also, if you are having trouble sleeping, an excellent work out can help release the tensions that are keeping you awake.

Yoga

Another form of exercise that can be very beneficial to your mind and body is yoga. This type of exercise can help to distribute some of your energies that have become stagnate. The meditative characteristics of yoga make it ideal for someone who is going through emotional difficulties.

Yoga is an exercise that requires a person to do body poses along with breathing techniques and meditation (Krans, 2018). The different yoga poses help a person to stretch and move their body in ways that increase the energy flow inside of their bodies. Combining these stretches with breathing techniques may help provide an outlet for any stress in the body. Because you must focus on breathing techniques and moving the body through a series of poses, yoga pulls the mind into the present.

Yoga is normally taught as a group activity. In class, a yoga instructor will assess the physical capabilities of the students and lead with group-appropriate poses. These poses are usually flexible and fluid in nature. A good yoga instructor will encourage the class to focus on positive images that will calm the body and the mind (Krans, 2016).

According to the Harvard Mental Health Letter, yoga can reduce stress; help with anxiety and depression; provide a self-soothing environment; and improve energy. Physiologically, it can also reduce your heart rate, lower blood pressure, ease breathing, and increase pain tolerance. As an exercise, yoga increases serotonin production, which studies suggest can help to eliminate depression (Krans, 2016). Yoga can also increase heart rate variability (HRV) by increasing the relaxation response over the stress response in the body. If your HRV is high, this means your body is adapting to stress (Krans, 2016). According to a study reported by Harvard Mental Health, people who were not stressed had a higher pain tolerance.

Hence, yoga is a popular exercise in hospitals as those who practice it develop an overall well-being, not just physical satisfaction. The meditative nature of yoga helps a person to achieve a mindfulness that they may not experience doing another type of exercise.

There are both pros and cons in using yoga for therapy. The pros are that yoga is safe when an instructor teaches you to do the poses properly. Additionally, yoga is beneficial for people who want better concentration, and yoga can easily be adapted for people with varying degrees of experience.

As a con, however, beginners and those with limited flexibility might find some of the poses to be difficult; depending on the pose, yoga may be uncomfortable or even physically painful. Yoga classes at private studios are oftentimes expensive. However, effort has been made to make yoga more accessible, and more classes are being taught at the YMCA, community centers, or through online classes.

Overall, yoga will reduce stress, anxiety, and depression. It is an exercise that promotes focus and controlled physical movements. Yoga is good for several types of people and can increase energy, improve sleep patterns, and relieve some types of pain.

Before beginning an exercise program, check with your doctor to make sure you are fit enough to do the exercise that you have chosen. Your doctor might also have some suggestions about exercise that can be very useful.

Meditation

Meditation is an altered state of consciousness that helps us to relax and be mindful of the present moment. It might be hard to become mindful during therapy, but meditation can help with doing so. There have been many studies that show how meditation can help reduce the symptoms of depression and anxiety, and in fact, research has found that those who meditate daily can actually physically change their brains. Specifically, "those who meditate daily can experience a breakdown in the neural connections in the brain that induce feelings of fear or anxiety" (Bell, 2019).

Meditation can also build connections in the brain that relate to empathy and the ability to assess problems rationally (Bell, 2019). A study conducted by Harvard Medical School found that within eight weeks of meditative practice, positive changes can be found in the brain. Meditation can also help to increase happiness and encourage contentment (McGreevey, 2019).

Even if you just practice meditation for ten minutes a day, you will see results. Your mind will function better, and symptoms of your depression will begin to dissolve as you work through your problems with a new focus.

Being able to slow down and just live in the present moment can help to erase some of the bad programming that happened during your relationship with the narcissist. It takes a keen sense of being present to be able to rise above the negative things ingrained into you by the narcissist, whose main skill seems to have been making you unhappy.

Practicing meditation and going to therapy can be very rewarding. Ask your therapist to help you find the type of mediation that is good for you. There are apps that are available for your smartphone that can help you achieve your goal of consistently meditating.

Massage Therapy

It is not uncommon to feel stressed when going through therapy or counseling. Focusing on some of the negatives in your life in order to change can be a daunting task, so it may be a good idea to try a soothing practice such as a professional massage.

A massage encourages relaxation and decreases tension and stress. When you get a proper massage, you release serotonin and dopamine, and you decrease your levels of cortisol ("Depression", 2019).

Cortisol is a hormone that is produced in response to stress. If you can lower this hormone, your body can produce more serotonin and better fight off pain, anxiety, and sadness. Releasing serotonin and dopamine can also help alleviate the symptoms of depression and improve your sleep cycle to better your overall health ("Massage", 2019).

When you get a massage, you are in a very safe place where you can relax, refocus, and find clarity. When you get a message, you are increasing the awareness of a mind-body connection. A safe, nurturing touch can fulfill your need for human contact with the added benefit of giving comfort and security. After all, receiving a good massage is akin to getting a big hug ("Massage, 2019).

It is important to work with a registered massage therapist because they can work with you to produce a treatment plan that will help decrease the symptoms of anxiety and depression. A good massage therapist will help you to create a sense of relief and empowerment, as well as establish a mind-body connection ("Massage", 2019).

Guided Imagery for Relaxation

Another method of achieving relaxation is to use guided imagery, which is a form of focused relaxation that helps create harmony between the mind and body ("Depression", 2019). By using guided imagery, you are coaching yourself on how to create a healthy and therapeutic mental escape. By being able to journey outside of what is causing you the most pain, you will better be able to cope. Sometimes you have to step out of something to be able to change it.

Overall, pursuing alternative therapies to enhance your well-being can be very rewarding. Engaging in an alternative therapy in addition to professional counseling can help you to move past the pain and anxiety of going no contact with the narcissist in a healthy manner. It will take a lot of adjustment for you to shed all the negativity that the narcissist has thrown your way, and when conventional therapy options are not enough, an alternative therapy aimed at enhancing your behavioral therapy session can have a very positive and profound effect on your progress.

Chapter Summary

- Alternative therapies can help to enhance your therapy sessions.

- There are different types of alternative therapies that can be good for you.

- Alternative can help you tolerate the emotional pain of your situation.

In the next chapter, you will learn how to avoid succumbing to another narcissistic relationship along with some methods to handle the narcissistic boss or coworker.

Chapter Ten: Learning to Change Patterns and Protect Yourself

The hardest step you had to take was to go no contact with the narcissist. You may have been able to break away completely; or, the narcissist may have been able to draw you back to him. If so, there is no shame in that. As we have discussed, leaving the narcissist when he deliberately presents himself as the ideal mate can be extremely difficult. However, do not feel discouraged. It is possible to achieve no contact and leave the narcissist.

If you are having trouble with the narcissist, there are steps that you can take to improve your situation. When he tries to argue with you, do not take the bait and disengage with the narcissist instead. You might feel tempted to confront the narcissist - if you could get through to him, you would not have to leave him. But as you know by now, you cannot cure a narcissist. No matter what you tell him, he will not believe you unless it supports his worldview.

Setting Up Boundaries

Set up boundaries that will help you not only in the present situation but in any future ones as well. The key to any boundary that you make is to be consistent. Do not set conditions that you will not be able to enforce. Start with something small like avoiding the places he frequents, and work to follow that plan consistently. When you are confident that you can keep the boundary, set another one.

If the narcissist crosses your boundary, call him on it. Enforce the limits you have drawn. Do not let the narcissist get away with provoking you, or else he will never take you seriously. Communicate to him the details of the boundary and the potential consequences if he breaks them. If you say you will call the police if he comes near you, do it – call the police. Do not panic if the narcissist tries to bluff his way through your conditions. Just stay firm and give out the consequence. Once you do this, the narcissist will think twice before he crosses a boundary with you again.

Eliminate Unhelpful Behaviors

A narcissist will tell you that what you are doing to him is not fair. Do not feel bad about this. The world is not fair. It was not fair when he treated you the way he did or put you through the things that he did. You are not perfect, and neither is he. You will no doubt partake in actions that the narcissist feels is unfair. Pay no attention to the narcissist's complaints and understand that his grievances are due to the fact that you are standing up for yourself (Grace, 2018).

Another concept that you need to do away with is always apologizing. When you apologize, the narcissist thinks that you are saying he is perfect (Grace, 2018). He does not see your apology as regret over your actions but instead thinks that you are admitting that he is right, and you are wrong.

You are a sensitive and empathic person; it feels right to apologize to remedy the other person's hurts. However, you must remember who you are dealing with: a person who would never say that he is sorry for his actions. The narcissist does not even understand the concept of apologizing.

Understanding the Reality of Your Situation

Diagnosing a person with NPD is a very serious thing. Moreover, there are different degrees of Narcissistic Personality

Disorder. You could decide that your narcissist is on the lower end of the spectrum or that she is on the higher end of it. Whatever you decide, know that you can not change her. She is who she is. It is a temptation to think that you can work with her narcissism, but in truth, the only person that could work with a narcissist would be a therapist who can teach the narcissist to become less self-centered. You cannot cure a narcissist. Accept that the narcissist and her behavior is not good for you.

If you must remain in contact with the narcissist, it is important that you remain firm in your belief that the narcissist will harm you. It may be tempting to rekindle your relationship after a long separation because she seems cured or better managed. This will not always be the case. In fact, if a narcissist says she is cured, ask to go to therapy with her and find out just how much progress the narcissist has made. Even then, you should not consider going back to him. Even if her condition has improved, she also has a habit of treating you poorly – a habit that even a therapist may not be able to change.

You need to accept who the narcissist is to you and move on from her. At first, it will be very painful, but as you progress into your recovering, you will understand more and more just what you were up against. And, hopefully, with better self-esteem, you will no longer succumb to the narcissist and her deception.

Things to Do to Protect Yourself

In the future, there might be a time that you attract yet another narcissist. They will be so charming and charismatic that you will not see the red flags in his personality right away. Yet as you get to know this person, you may start to suspect he suffers from NPD. Don't panic as there are things you can do to protect yourself and rid this new narcissist from your life.

The first thing that you need to do is recognize that this new person is a narcissist. He does not have to be a love interest; he may be a friend, coworker, or family member. Regardless of the narcissist's role in your life, you need to be strong and realize that this person is not healthy for you. Realizing that this person is a narcissist before you engage in a relationship with them can save you a lot of grief in the future.

In dealing with a narcissist, you need to separate fact from fiction. Does this person do what he or she says they are going to do? Does this person brag a lot but do very little? If the latter is true, it may be a sign that you are dealing with someone who has a large ego with a lot of insecurity. Remember, narcissists have a grandiose idea of who they are. With experience, you will be able to see through the over-blown character of the narcissist and not participate in any of his falsehoods.

When you have to deal with the narcissist on a regular basis, watch what you say. If he or she is a coworker or family member, you may have to see them on a daily basis. Learn what triggers the narcissist and stay away from those topics. Remember that you do not have to engage with the narcissist and work on his social skills or ethics. If you must interact with him or her, remain calm and extricate yourself from the situation when possible. Narcissists do not like to be challenged; they do not like to take responsibility for their actions. Trying to help the narcissist may only make things worse. Walk away from tricky situations, and let the narcissist tend to whatever they are tangled up in.

Future Relationships

One of the things that you can work on is determining the patterns in the relationships that you seek out. Do you primarily end up with people that are on the narcissistic spectrum?

Write down all the relationships that you have had and rate them on how many narcissistic qualities they may have. You might begin to see a pattern. Perhaps you had never been involved with a narcissist before this last relationship. Or perhaps you have a history of gravitating towards narcissists. Now rate the intensity of the narcissists that you were involved with. Are there any commonalities. For example, are the narcissists all part of the same spectrum? Can they all be placed in the mild, intense, or middle ranges of the spectrum?

This informal survey can be very helpful to you, especially if you want to break the pattern of getting involved with a narcissist. Once you see a pattern, you will be able to begin to change your expectations for people that you are going to be involved with. You will be able to set some boundaries and avoid future abuse and suffering.

Becoming a Stronger Person

Narcissists hate to be with someone who is going to call their bluff or challenge them. While you are in recovery, you will become a stronger person. The type of person who is not needy and weak. You will become a person who can not be gaslighted or any of the other antics that a narcissist will use on you.

A narcissist is not going to be involved with a strong woman who knows her mind. Therefore, develop yourself to be a strong and authentic. When you meet a narcissist, call them on their behavior and challenge them to be real instead of fake.

When they can not do this, move on, and do not get involved with them again.

Connect with Yourself

Develop yourself as an authentic person. Be the strong person you have always dreamed of being. Stop letting fear dictate your actions. Be confident in your choices, and do not let anyone sway you into thinking that you can't think for yourself. A narcissist will not like that there is nothing he can use to manipulate you with. There are no holes or weakness that he can twist to his advantage. Stop being vulnerable with every person. Choose wisely the persons that you are going to discuss your shortcomings with. Beware of the narcissist because he lives to use these kinds of things to his advantage.

Stop Trying to Save People

When you meet a person on the narcissist spectrum, do not believe that you can help the person get over their NPD. Let them face their own problems. Remind yourself that you want a healthy relationship, not a codependent one. Let the narcissist go to therapy on their own. You do not have to drag them there, nor do you have to become that person's therapist, however.

Do not feel like you have to rescue the narcissist. You need to emotionally detach from the people you meet that are on the narcissistic spectrum. The narcissist will try to get you to absorb pain and blame. Do not do that for any person – at any time.

You no longer have to rescue people to prove anything to yourself. Your job is to be an authentic person and find other fruitful ways to grow your self-esteem and self-worth. You need to cultivate your own feelings of value and safety. Furthermore, stop looking to others for validation. It is self-defeating to try to get a narcissistic person to validate you. They have an interest in keeping you weak and feeling like a failure. Learn to validate yourself and stop giving others the power to tell you if you are doing something right or wrong.

Do Not Get Involved in Another Narcissistic Relationship

As you become a stronger person, you will not be as attractive to a narcissist as you once were. However, there are a lot of people who are on the narcissistic spectrum. Even though you are cautious, it is good to take steps that will ward off any narcissist who tries to become involved with you.

Make sure to ask the new person as many questions as they ask you.

Narcissists live to collect information about you, but they give little information about themselves in return. If you notice that someone is repeating what you just said, be cautious about him or her. For example, you might say that you love romantic movies, and they respond with "So do I." Instead of accepting this as an answer, ask them to name a specific romantic movie that they like. This will let the narcissist know that you are not an easy target.

Be wary when revealing personal information.

A narcissist asks your personal questions so that he can get close to you as soon as possible. The narcissist wants to cut corners in building a relationship, and this is not a good thing. Also, revealing anything too personal will leave you open for attack in the future. The narcissist will always use your vulnerabilities against you.

Maintain your alone time.

A narcissist will want to spend every waking minute with you in the beginning. He will blast you with attention in order to control you. By sending you a lot of texts and emails, he is breaking into your time. If you go out somewhere to be alone, like a peaceful walk, do not answer the phone. The narcissist is stealing your time away from you and trying to control you.

Don't change your routine.

When you meet someone that wants to take you away from your routine, be very cautious. It is important that no one takes away the time that you spend with your friends and family. If you have a regular movie night with someone, the narcissist will try to see you on that night. Stay away from the person who only wants to do things with you and not anyone else. A narcissist wants to isolate you so that you become dependent on him or her. Keep up your routines, and do not change them for anyone, no matter how compelling an argument they give you.

Get comfortable with your boundaries.

Boundaries are what keep you safe and happy. It's not good to have not have any boundaries when you are a sensitive and feeling person. You might be under the impression that you need to always put yourself out there and be genuine. In fact, you feel that in order to get to know someone, you need to let down your guard. But while it seems like being relaxed is the best thing for an empathetic person, it is not. You need boundaries so that people do not take advantage of you. If you meet a narcissist, he or she will try to tear down your boundaries and quickly establish intimacy so that they can move on to taking advantage of you. But if you have strong boundaries, it is almost certain that you will repel any narcissist that you meet.

These are some of the things that you need to do in order to protect yourself from getting involved with a narcissist again. Do not fear that you will fall back into your old habits and attract another narcissist. Now that you have learned more about the covert narcissist, you will be more aware of meeting another one again. Have confidence in yourself.

Narcissists in the Workplace

Once you become familiar with the characteristics of a narcissistic relationship, you might find narcissists in other parts of your life. Specifically, you may find that you work with a narcissist. How will you know if your boss or co-worker is a narcissist?

The narcissist in your workplace can have an attitude of superiority or a belief that if it was not for him, the workplace would fall apart. The narcissist may be the type of person who always rushes to help in situations where he is not needed. He does this because he thinks only he can solve the problem, not anyone else. These types of narcissists think they are saints who have unrealistic views of their abilities (Chen, 2017).

The Two Types of Workplace Narcissists

The two different types of narcissists found in the workplace are agentic narcissists and communal narcissists. The agentic narcissist is the type of person that thinks he is superior to other people in the office. He is arrogant and rarely waits to hear any other person's ideas or solutions. The communal narcissist, on the other hand, is a martyr. He is a self-appointed saint with unrealistic views about his efforts in the workplace. In other words, he believes that he is the only one in the office that is keeping things together (Chen, 2017).

Whether your coworker is an agentic or communal narcissist, it is still possible to work together. Delegate certain projects to him, and let him have his own little world where he can call all the shots. Encourage the communal narcissist to work with as many teams as possible. The more people he feels he has helped, the better the workplace environment will be. However, be sure that other team members get recognized for their efforts as well. This will prevent the workplace narcissist from taking all the credit.

It is important that you understand that, similar to any other narcissist, you will never be able to change the workplace narcissist. Still, there are some things you can do to lessen his impact at the workplace (Lamberg, 2019).

Ignore the narcissist

Although you may want to call out the narcissist, the best thing to do is to ignore the behavior and resist the urge to engage in a power struggle. Just attend to your own work and give the narcissist all the space that he needs.

Spot the gaslighting effect

The workplace narcissist is going to want to diminish you and get all the attention and credit. He will question your version of an event or make your concerns seem trivial. He might even be abusive when you work with him but twist the abuse and make it your fault. Such things are classic gaslighting moves. Hold fast to your knowledge that the narcissist is gaslighting you, and do not engage with him.

Do not challenge

Do not challenge the workplace narcissist. There will be situations in the workplace when the narcissist thinks he has the definitive answer for a problem. If you challenge him in front of others, he will implode, and then try to punish you. So, it is best not to challenge the workplace narcissist. Find a way to express yourself that will not make the workplace narcissist feel challenged.

Understand the narcissist and his insecurity

Although the narcissist might look to be the most confident person in the room, he is not. Remember that the narcissist is suffering from a mental disorder. His actions come from an insecure place. Have some compassion for the narcissist, but keep your distance.

Be firm about boundaries

An effective way to survive a workplace narcissist is to have very firm boundaries with him. Make him understand that you will not engage in arguments and that you will not let him manipulate situations that push your boundaries. Understand that the narcissist cannot be trusted and that he does not have the communication skills to participate in a healthy relationship with you. Do not let the workplace narcissist trample on your boundaries.

Ask for help

Unlike a romantic relationship, there are others involved with the workplace narcissist. It may be helpful if you join with other coworkers in learning to deal with the workplace narcissist. Share with each other strategies that have worked when dealing with him. In an unobtrusive way, ask the advice of your coworkers and seek out their support. No one person will be able to change the narcissist, but sometimes sharing the burden of working with the narcissist can be very helpful.

Lessons Learned

When trying to get over your narcissistic relationship, it might be overwhelming to realize there are other narcissists in your life. The last place you want to deal with a narcissist is your workplace or family. However, let the fact that you are learning new skills that will help you deal with these other narcissists. It can also be helpful to observe other people and see how they deal with the narcissist. Knowing that you are not the only one dealing with a narcissist can bring you some comfort.

Chapter Summary

- Write down your past relationships and look for patterns
- Become a strong person and authentic person to repel narcissists
- It is possible to stay out of a narcissistic relationship

Final Words

The journey to recovery will have ups and downs, but you will reach a point where you are better again. It is natural for you to feel angry at the narcissist. He or she hurt you on a level that you have never experienced before. You might even be tempted to be angry at yourself for getting involved with a narcissist. Don't despair and suppress all of that anger. Let it out. Do something positive to work through that anger, such as an exercise program that helps you to release this anger. Trying something peaceful like yoga or taking long walks is ideal.

Asking for help is the next step in your recovery. It is hard to do something as complicated as getting over a narcissist. The narcissist was very hurtful, and the trauma of his actions towards you needs to be dealt with. Don't suffer in silence; get a therapist, or open up to a trusted friend. There is no reason for you to try to heal on your own. The narcissist used many manipulative tricks on you like gaslighting you and blaming you for things you did not do. You need someone else to help you rewrite the negative thoughts that resulted from your traumatic relationship.

Stick with the no contact rule. It is not good for you to be around the narcissist when you are trying to heal. There is no good reason for interacting with the narcissist again. If you share friends, now is an appropriate time to make new friends. If you share family, detach yourself when you have to see the narcissist. The best thing you can do is to take away any reason for the narcissist to talk or get involved with you again. If you need to go to a lawyer to draw up a modified plan of contact, do so. Do not be afraid of getting a restraining order against the narcissist if necessary. You need to protect yourself at all costs. Enforce any legal actions, and do not let the narcissist off the hook. If you let him get away with anything, he will feel vindicated and try to get close to you once again. This is the last thing you need to deal with in your recovery.

It's okay to stop learning about the narcissist and abusive relationships. You have reached a point where your recovery is the most important thing. You no longer have to dwell on what the narcissist did to you. Instead, you need to work on building your authentic self so that you can repel any other narcissist that come your way. Fill your head with healing thoughts and become self-centered for a little while as you are healing. It's okay to put yourself first. It is important in recovery that you treat yourself as well as you can.

Now is the time to work on your self-esteem. Build yourself up instead of tearing yourself down. This is the time that you need to wipe out all the negative things the narcissist ever told you. Consider learning some grounding techniques or self-soothing methods. Even though you are at a low point, remember that there are things that you can do for yourself. Replace the negative things with the positives in your life. Remember who you were before you met the narcissist. You have not changed. The good stuff was beaten out of you by relentless belittling and abuse. Now is the time to reacquaint yourself with the best parts of you. They are still there. And, as you heal, you will create even more good qualities.

Do things that are healing. Don't just read books about healing. Instead, get out and meet new people that are positive. Do activities that make you feel better about yourself. Try a new hobby that will help you to keep your mind off of the narcissist. Fretting over whether or not the narcissist is thinking about you or regrets losing you is not a healing activity. If you have something to occupy your mind, you will not have the time to think of the narcissist. Exercising and eating healthy will boost your healing to a higher level. By taking care of your body, you will be able to take care of your mind.

Get in touch with your spiritual self, and find peace in meditation. At first, it might be difficult to clear your head of negative thoughts. In fact, it might be too hard to sit down and meditate for any length of time. What you need to do is start with a short span of time and increase it every day. Meditation helps you to become mindful. When you are mindful, you live in the present and not in the future or the past. This is a very important step in your healing. Living in the past will cause you to reinforce the negative things that the narcissist would say and do. And, living in the future can overwhelm you. So, it is best to just be mindful and get comfortable with your present self.

Recovering from your abusive relationship with a narcissist is no small task, but it will become natural to you after a period of time. Make good habits, like being mindful and being positive. Do things that refresh you and make you stronger. Stay away from people who are negative and make you feel bad about yourself. This could mean that you need to make new friends. Be firm with your family, and help them to understand what kind of positive interactions they can have with you.

Above all, be true to yourself. There is no one that you have to please besides yourself. Let the narcissist be part of your past and not part of your present and future. It might be hard for you at first, but every day, you will grow stronger. Don't doubt that you will recover and be even stronger and more authentic as a result of healing. Be confident that your future will be bright. The worst is behind you, and the best is straight ahead.

A note from the author:

Did you enjoy reading this book? Please consider leaving it a review so that I can continue to put out more content like this! Thank you for this important contribution. Also remember to explore the other books in this four part series, "Empath Awakening," a helpful guide for sensitive people, "Toxic Magnetism," an exploration into the root cause of attraction to narcissists, and "Am I Codependent?" a book devoted entirely to recovery from codependency.

References

Alternative Therapies for Depression. (n.d.). Retrieved from https://my.clevelandclinic.org/health/treatments/9303-depression-alternative-therapies.

American Psychiatric Association. (2000). *Diagnostic and statistical manual of mental disorders* (4th ed., text rev.). Washington, DC: Author.

American Psychiatric Association. (2013). *Diagnostic and statistical manual of mental disorders* (5th ed.). Washington, DC: Author.

Audible Studios on Brilliance audio. (2017). *Becoming the Narcissists Nightmare How to Devalue and Discard the Narcissist While Supplying Yourself.*

Arabi, S. (2018, August 10). Research Finds That Narcissists Try To Remain Friends With Their Exes For Darker Reasons. Retrieved from https://blogs.psychcentral.com/recovering-narcissist/2018/08/research-finds-that-narcissists-try-to-remain-friends-with-their-exes-for-darker-reasons/.

Arabi, S. (2016). *Becoming the Narcissist Nightmare:* . SCW Archer Publishing.

Bell, G. (2017, November 29). What it's like to meditate with depression. Retrieved from https://www.headspace.com/blog/2017/11/04/meditating-with-depression/.

Cherry, K. (2019, July 15). How Behavioral Therapy Is Used in Psychology. Retrieved from https://www.verywellmind.com/what-is-behavioral-therapy-2795998.

Catalog, T. (2017, December 18). How to heal from the toxic triangulation of narcissists. Retrieved from https://www.salon.com/2017/12/18/how-to-heal-from-the-toxic-triangulation-of-narcissists_partner/.

Esposito, L. (2015, Feb 6). Forget Co-Parenting with a Narcissist. Do This Instead. Retrieved from https://www.psychologytoday.com/us/blog/anxiety-zen/201502/forget-co-parenting-narcissist-do-instead.

Fritscher, L. (2018, May 14). How Individual Therapy Works. Retrieved from https://www.verywellmind.com/individual-therapy-2671605.

Galan, N. (2019, February 26). 8 herbs and supplements to help treat depression. Retrieved from https://www.medicalnewstoday.com/articles/314421.php.

Greenberg, E. (2018, July 28). How Do I Heal from Narcissistic Abuse? Retrieved from https://www.psychologytoday.com/us/blog/understanding-narcissism/201807/how-do-i-heal-narcissistic-abuse.

Herbal Medicine. (n.d.). Retrieved from https://www.hopkinsmedicine.org/health/wellness-and-prevention/herbal-medicine.

Hurd, S., Hurd, S., Sherrie, Hurd, S., Sherrie, Hansen, T., ... Fiona. (2019, May 1). 7 Things a Covert Narcissist Mother Does to Her Children. Retrieved from https://www.learning-mind.com/covert-narcissist-mother-signs/.

Kartha, D. (2018, June 3). Narcissistic Rage. Retrieved from https://psychologenie.com/narcissistic-rage.

Kassel, G. (2019, January 30). 11 Signs You're Dating a Narcissist - and How to Get Out. Retrieved from https://www.healthline.com/health/mental-health/am-i-dating-a-narcissist.

Krans, B. (2016, Aug 15). Using Yoga to Relieve the Symptoms of Depression. Retrieved from https://www.healthline.com/health/depression/yoga-therapy#pros-and-cons.

Lamberg, E. (n.d.). 7 Ways to Deal with a Toxic Narcissist at Work. *Reader's Digest*. Retrieved from https://www.rd.com/advice/relationships/toxic-narcissist/.

Lancer, D. (2018, Feb 18). Daughters of Narcissistic Mothers. Retrieved from https://www.psychologytoday.com/us/blog/toxic-relationships/201802/daughters-narcissistic-mothers.

McGreevey, S. (2019, September 12). Eight weeks to a better brain. Retrieved from https://news.harvard.edu/gazette/story/2011/01/eight-weeks-to-a-better-brain/.

Narcissistic personality disorder. (2017, November 18). Retrieved from https://www.mayoclinic.org/diseases-conditions/narcissistic-personality-disorder/symptoms-causes/syc-20366662.

Narcissists and the No Contact Rule. (n.d.). Retrieved from https://psychologia.co/narcissist-no-contact/

Never had a massage? What you should know. (2018, October 6). Retrieved from https://www.mayoclinic.org/healthy-lifestyle/stress-management/in-depth/massage/art-20045743.

Orloff, J. (2018). *The empaths survival guide: life strategies for sensitive people.* Boulder, CO: Sounds True, Inc.

Phatak, R. (2018, March 26). Overt Vs. Covert Narcissism: A Quick Comparison. Retrieved from https://psychologenie.com/overt-vs-covert-narcissism.

Powell, W. (2016, Oct 1). 10 Key Ways To Avoid The Trap Of Dating A Narcissist. (2018, June 24). Retrieved from https://thoughtcatalog.com/g00/wendy-powell/2016/10/10-key-ways-to-avoid-the-trap-of-dating-a-narcissist/?i10c.ua=1&i10c.encReferrer=aHR0cHM6Ly93d3cuZ29vZ2xlLmNvbS8=&i10c.dv=22.

Schimelpfening, N. (2019, September 1). How to Decide Which Type of Therapy to Seek for Treating Depression. Retrieved from https://www.verywellmind.com/types-of-psychotherapy-for-depression-1067407.

www.ingramcontent.com/pod-product-compliance
Lightning Source LLC
Chambersburg PA
CBHW060032040426
42333CB00042B/2317